VICTORIA & ALBERT MUSEUM

GEORGIAN FURNITURE

Introduction by
RALPH EDWARDS, C.B.E., F.S.A.

LONDON: HER MAJESTY'S STATIONERY OFFICE
1958

LARGE PICTURE BOOK No. 1
First published 1947
Second Edition 1958

Sold at the
Victoria & Albert Museum, South Kensington,
and by Her Majesty's Stationery Office,
at the addresses given on page 3 of cover.

Printed in Great Britain by
W. S. Cowell Ltd,
The Butter Market, Ipswich.

FOREWORD

THIS PICTORIAL SURVEY of Georgian furniture was made by Mr Ralph Edwards when he was Keeper of the Department of Woodwork, and his introduction was adapted from the fourth volume of the Museum's *Catalogue of English Furniture and Woodwork* which has long been out of print. This new edition of *Georgian Furniture* has been revised to include material acquired by the Museum since 1950, including objects from Osterley Park.

August 1957   TRENCHARD COX
                                                                  Director

GEORGIAN FURNITURE

THIS volume provides a general pictorial survey of the Museum collection of English furniture between the years 1720–1820. Throughout the period, furniture was designed in relation to interior decoration, which in its turn was most intimately related to its architectural environment. The series of Georgian panelled rooms in the Museum serves to suggest this decorative background, but a comprehensive view of its development must be sought in the diminishing number of town and country houses of the Augustan age which still retain their original character. The contents of Osterley – pronounced by Horace Walpole to be 'the palace of palaces', with a drawing-room 'worthy of Eve before the fall' – are the property of the Museum; and there we are able to realize the full measure of Robert Adam's achievement (Figs. 5, 6 and 7).

The century between the death of Queen Anne and the accession of George IV is marked by rapid growth and development in English national life. Before it closed, the traditional organization of society, dating back to the Middle Ages, had yielded to urbanization and industrial enterprise based upon machinery. This change, known as the Industrial Revolution, had a far-reaching effect upon all the applied arts, and inaugurated an era of mass production. The restless enquiring spirit of the eighteenth century finds expression in its decoration and furniture. It was a time of creative energy and ceaseless experiment. Within its limits several distinct styles, inspired by conflicting ideals, rose and waned. To each a fickle and capricious society accorded a welcome soon to be withdrawn. There was an avid demand for novelties and the latest mode. Baroque extravagance gave way to rococo fantasy, and that to a refined classicism, which, at the end of the century, was superseded by an archaeological revival based on a close study of the remains of the ancient world.

DECORATION AND WOODWORK

In the great Palladian houses of the Early Georgian period the decorative treatment associated with the later English Renaissance and Sir Christopher Wren was largely transformed by Italian influence. This movement owed much to cultured and travelled amateurs, like Richard Boyle, third Earl of Burlington, while Colin Campbell's *Vitruvius Britannicus* (1717) sums up its aims. The state rooms in houses built by Campbell, Kent, Leoni, Brettingham and others versed in this Italianate style, were of great size and height. In them a lavish use was made of decorative painting, stucco and marble. The vogue for the baroque painted

5

decoration introduced by Verrio and his school in Charles II's reign persisted into the succeeding age, and ceilings continued to be adorned with naked deities and allegorical subjects, which are often distinguished by great facility and brilliance of handling. When panelling was introduced, instead of the wide bolection mouldings of the previous age, the panels were 'fielded', *i.e.* chamfered at the edges and set in a plain framework, or recessed within carved borders. Cedar, walnut, and mahogany (as at Houghton for Sir Robert Walpole) were sometimes employed, but early in George III's reign, according to the architect Isaac Ware, deal or pine had become 'almost the universal timber'.

In these panelled rooms decoration was concentrated on the salient features. The chimney-pieces, of marble or carved wood, with architraves, pilasters or terminal figures supporting the mantelshelf, continue the tradition of Inigo Jones; indeed, some of them were almost transcripts of his designs. These chimney-pieces are often found with an upper stage enclosing a picture. The doorways have richly moulded surrounds and a convex frieze with central tablet supporting a pediment.

Alcoves and wall niches are freely introduced, while the pine woodwork was invariably painted, olive green, blue, buff and brown being the colours most commonly employed. Later, white of a shade approaching ivory was considerably used, the salient detail being enriched with gilding. This type of Georgian interior is well represented in the Museum by the room from Hatton Garden (Fig. 1), which conforms to the rule laid down by Abraham Swan that 'there must be sufficient spaces left plain so that the ornament in proper places may be more conspicuous and may have their desired effect'. This room and another rather less ornate example from Great George Street (Fig. 2) were stripped of successive layers of paint, which obscured the carving, soon after they had been acquired; but have since been repainted.

In many great houses the walls of state rooms were of painted plaster with lavish enrichments of masks, festoons and trophies executed, mainly by Italian stuccoists, in bold relief, the upper stage of the chimney-piece being decorated in stucco or marble with figure compositions adapted from classic originals. Walls were also hung with damask, velvet and tapestry; while papers printed from wooden blocks, or with the designs drawn and coloured by hand, were popular as a cheaper substitute. Some of these papers were copied from Chinese originals, and a room from Wooton-under-Edge, Gloucestershire, dating from about 1740, is an example of highly skilful imitation. A specimen of the Chinese papers from which such copies derive, formerly at Moor Park, is now exhibited in Room 126. Some of the best known cabinet-makers of the period carried out interior decoration on a considerable scale: thus, Chippendale's bills contain many items for supplying wallpapers.

From about the middle of the century, rococo influence becomes perceptible in the carved enrichments and stucco decoration of 'houses of consequence'. They lose their heavy baroque character, becoming noticeably lighter and more fanciful in treatment. The 'capricious ornament' against which Colin Campbell had inveighed was carried much further and became the mode. Interlaced scrolls in endless variety with a medley of naturalistic ornament – rocks and shells, foliage, and flowers – formed the decorative repertory of this new style, which derived from the *rocaille* of Pineau, Cuvillier, Meissonier, and other contemporary French designers. Highly sophisticated, despite its apparent resort to nature, it aimed at a kind of logical disorder and the consistent exploitation of asymmetric curves.

French inspiration is very apparent in the lavishly carved and gilded enrichments of the splendid Music Room (Fig. 3) which was presented to the Museum in 1938, on the demolition of Norfolk House, St James's Square. Its decoration recalls that of the contemporary drawing-room formerly at Chesterfield House, Mayfair, which was built by Isaac Ware for the fourth Earl of Chesterfield and completed in 1752.

In the closely related 'Chinese taste', used experimentally in lesser rooms, the extreme of bizarre invention is attained. Sir William Chambers, the first English architect to visit China, sought to suppress the wilder manifestations of this exotic craze – 'the extravagant fancies that daily appear under the name of Chinese'. The Gothic style, a travesty of medieval art applied to structures of lath and plaster, was taken up by Horace Walpole and a group of dilettanti of whom Richard Bentley and 'that great genius', Sanderson Miller, were the most influential. It soon found its way into pattern books, and the 'bastard Gothic' of such designers as Batty Langley, for all its essential absurdity, possesses a kind of preposterous charm.

About 1760, these strange aberrations gave way before a newly wakened enthusiasm for classical remains, evoked by the discoveries at Pompeii and Herculaneum and by such publications as Stuart and Revett's *Antiquities* (1762). The dominant spirit in this movement was Robert Adam, who, soon after his return from Italy in 1758, effected a complete revolution in architecture and the allied arts. He substituted for the ponderous conceptions of the Palladian school a decorative convention based on the remains of Greek and Roman buildings, and on the grotesques and arabesques of Cinquecento ornament – all adapted to new purposes with astonishing resource. Though Sir William Chambers, James Wyatt, James Paine, Thomas Leverton, and other fashionable architects embraced these classical ideals, Adam's ascendancy was such that within a brief period 'everything was Adamitic, buildings and furniture of every description'. The effect upon interior decoration was profound. A complete harmony was obtained in the design of the ceiling and walls, the pattern of the carpet, the furniture and fittings, everything being brought within the compass of a single style, logically conceived, and consistently worked out. Halls, and principal living-rooms were often circular or elliptical, broken up by large alcoves, and with ceilings domed, vaulted, or groined. Stucco decoration was now executed with extreme delicacy and finish, the designs drawing freely upon the repertory of classic ornament collected from Italian encaustic paintings and bas-reliefs. This light and elegant 'Grecian' treatment provoked some protests from the admirers of the more virile 'Roman' manner, and was stigmatized by Sir William Chambers as 'filigrane toy-work'.

Decorative painting was brought into the closest stylistic harmony with the plaster enrichments, imparting warmth and colour to rooms. The compartments of ceilings, overdoors, and panels were filled with classic subjects, arabesque designs of Renaissance character being also used with excellent effect. As at the beginning of the century, most of the best decorative artists were Italians: Zucchi, Cipriani, Bonomi, Biagio Rebecca, and Angelica Kauffmann all obtaining wide patronage in England.

Mass production is already foreshadowed in some of the processes employed. Much of the plaster ornament was cast from moulds; scagliola, an imitation of coloured marbles in composition, was used for columns and floors, while marbling and graining were resorted to, at the close of the period, to enhance the effect of inferior woods. Sporadic attempts were made, however, to revive the ambitious mural painting of earlier times. John Mortimer carried out an elaborate scheme of decoration on the coved ceiling of the saloon at Brocket Hall, Herts., the work being completed after his death by Francis Wheatley. At Drakelowe Hall, Derbyshire, Paul Sandby decorated the walls of the dining-room with mountainous landscapes and foliage in *gouache*. The alcove end of this room, dated 1793, is now in the Museum. These are rare instances of true mural painting. Most of this late eighteenth-century decoration consists of canvases painted in the studio and let into the ceiling or applied to the walls. It was an age of substitutes, and much of its ornament violated the nature of the material imitated; composition strengthened with metal cores allowing of a delicacy of treatment impossible in carved wood.

Refined simplicity is the keynote of interior decoration in the last years of the century. It is seen at its best in the work of the brilliant architect, Henry Holland, who between 1795 and 1800 built Southill for Samuel Whitbread and enlarged Carlton House for the Prince Regent. Holland may be held to have introduced the French version of classicism favoured by the Prince and his circle. He had an almost infallible sense of proportion, and a remarkable power of imparting fresh life to a decorative convention already outworn.

With the end of the century the influence of the French *directoire* style achieved a final victory over the lingering Renaissance tradition, represented by the later followers of Adam. A new and more intense study of classical precedents set in. A Greek revival was sponsored by architects, while Egyptian remains were added to the sources of inspiration. Napoleon's African campaign and Denon's great work, *Voyage dans la Basse et la Haute Egypte* (1802), helped to establish this vogue; but it was discouraged by Thomas Hope, the leading English designer of decoration and furniture who warned its votaries that as Egyptian symbolism was 'seldom intelligible' in ordinary households, it should be sparingly used. This revived enthusiasm for the antique produced a frigid, pedantic style with a strong bias towards archaeology. The free use of enrichments in interior decoration was considered frivolous and ruthlessly suppressed by the more austere protagonists of the movement; Sir John Soane pronouncing that ornaments appropriate to the temples of the ancients 'became puerile and disgusting in English houses'. Under this ban, cornices, columns, and entablatures were often included; so that such interiors, stripped of traditional structural elements, now present a meagre and forbidding aspect. At the time, this appearance was mitigated by wallpapers and window draperies, often in primary colours and decorated with Greek, Roman, or Egyptian patterns. Few of these still survive to give an adequate impression of this strange archaeological style, which its votaries held to be the final expression of civilized and enlightened taste.

FURNITURE

Some years after the death of Queen Anne the simple and dignified furniture associated with her reign was superseded by a new style, baroque in conception and based upon French and Italian models. On the repeal of the heavy import duties, mahogany from the West Indies gradually replaced walnut as the fashionable material. Gilding was freely used to enhance carved ornament, while the ostentatious mirrors, side-tables, and stands characteristic of the period were of pinewood overlaid with gesso and gilt.* This grandiose style was developed by architects for a small governing class, and was at first confined to a few palatial houses. Among the chief structural elements are columns, architraves, and entablatures, with terminal figures and heavy scrolled supports. Favourite ornaments are swags and wreaths of flowers, lion and human masks, and broadly handled acanthus leaves. The chief exponent of this new manner of furnishing was William Kent (1684–1748), who, after studying in Italy, was introduced to the fashionable world by the third Earl of Burlington. He soon became an arbiter of taste and achieved a reputation in several branches of art. Kent was the first Englishman to bring movable furniture within the scope of his architectural schemes. He designed not only houses but much of their contents for the Duke of Devonshire and the Earls of Burlington and Leicester; while elsewhere he was responsible for a great part of the interior, though another architect had been employed. At Holkham, Houghton, and Rousham, his furniture may still be seen in the setting for which it was carefully thought out. Planned to harmonize with Palladian architecture and baroque decoration, it is incongruous, at least in its more extravagant forms, when associated with other styles. Characteristic of Kent's style is the monumental side-table from Coleshill (Fig. 14). The Museum also possesses the two sarcophagus-like chests (Figs. 12 and 13), the eagle side-table (Fig. 15) and a mirror probably designed by him for Frederick, Prince of Wales (Fig. 73).

Some of the earliest engraved designs for furniture published in England conform to this style and illustrate it in a modified form adapted to the homes of the middle classes. Among the most important are the designs for side-tables, cabinets, and bookcases given in Batty and Thomas Langley's *City and Country Workmen's Treasury*. These designs are dated 1739, and with others issued about the same time are the productions of minor architects or builders. They are merely complementary to the architecture illustrated and suggest no technical knowledge; indeed, two of Langley's side-tables are exact transcripts from designs by Nicholas Pineau, the celebrated French sculptor and decorative artist. The side-table (Fig. 16) is based on the designs in the *Treasury*, Plates CXLII-CXLIII.

The names of a number of the more prominent craftsmen of the Early Georgian period have been handed down to us, mainly through the preservation of their bills. John Gumley, a well-known cabinetmaker and glass manufacturer, was in partnership with James Moore between 1714 and 1726, the firm carrying on business in the Strand. It supplied the Royal palaces with mirrors, chandeliers, frames for tables, and a variety of gilt and walnut furniture. The word 'Gumley' is carved on the frame of one of the tall, gilt wall mirrors at Hampton Court Palace; while Moore's name appears on a set, consisting of a gilt gesso table and candlesticks, also at the Palace. Such inscriptions are rare on English furniture of the eighteenth century, though printed trade labels, advertising the makers' wares, are

* The process employed throughout the eighteenth century is known as 'water gilding'. On a thick skin of size and whiting, a coating of clay, generally red or blue, was laid. After it had been rubbed down and moistened with water the gold leaf was applied to this ground. In the later oil gilding process a preparation of boiled oil (gold size) is used instead of water. This process is cheaper and more expeditious, but oil gilding discolours in a comparatively brief time. In gesso gilding the surface was thickly coated with the preparation, in which the more delicate ornament was carved. A remarkable example of original water gilding, until lately preserved by coats of paint, can be seen in the Early Georgian mirror (Fig. 74). Oil gilding of mirror frames is allowed by Stalker and Parker (*Treatise of Japanning and Varnishing*, 1688) and the accounts show that it was practised in the decoration of Ham House in 1638.

sometimes found affixed to cabinets, chests of drawers, and tables. Reliable attributions can be made to Moore on stylistic grounds as his furniture is highly idiosyncratic. A side-table decorated with gilt gesso and bearing the arms of Richard, first Lord Cobham (Fig. 10) has the variety of pillar leg and carved stretcher which Moore particularly favoured. A marriage coffer of sarcophagus form (Fig. 12) is a most characteristic example of the lavish baroque phase, and here some of the decorative motives are also reminiscent of Moore. Benjamin Goodison, of the Golden Spread Eagle in Long Acre, was largely employed by the Crown in George II's reign, and to him may be attributed the mirror made for the Prince of Wales (Fig. 73). The side-table, which was formerly at Stowe, reminds us that the baroque was established in favour before Kent's return from Italy in 1719.

Towards the middle of the century this ponderous style gave way to one which was its complete antithesis. Something has been said above of rococo decoration, and a similar indulgence in caprice and fancy distinguishes the furniture of that age. Among the earliest indications of the change are the designs for mirrors and wall-lights, published by Mathias Lock about 1745, in which the lively spirit of French *rocaille* is cleverly rendered. Lock was a draughtsman of rare ability and is now recognized as the pioneer of rococo in England. But it is in the first edition of Chippendale's *Director* (1754) that the new style is seen fully naturalized and combined with excursions into the contemporary Gothic and Chinese 'tastes'. Recent research has thrown a flood of light upon the genesis of this famous trade catalogue, with the result that Chippendale's personal responsibility must be heavily discounted. Lock and his collaborator, H. Copeland, who were in Chippendale's employ at the time, were undoubtedly responsible for the majority of the designs. Those in the rococo style are largely derivative, owing much to the leading French decorative artists, but in the process of adaptation they acquired an unmistakable national idiom. Many extravagant fancies remained unrealized, or were freely modified in the course of manufacture. Lacking the audacity and invention of the *rocaille*, a certain good sense and sobriety characterizes most of the English versions. The more resolute attempts to emulate French exuberance are represented by a commode acquired in 1957. Among the examples which represent the style in its more coherent and successful form are two fine mirrors (Fig. 81), which are probably from Chippendale's workshop; while the tea table (Fig. 21), with its faultless proportions and delicate ornament, shows that at the height of rococo influence, elegant simplicity was sometimes achieved.

In range and variety the *Director* represented a new departure, for it included not only ceremonial furniture but a great variety of types for ordinary domestic use. Some of the most important designs were intended to be gilt and japanned. Of this treatment the japanned bedstead from Badminton (Fig. 9) is a capital instance. It shows, moreover, the Chinese vogue 'in its most advanced degree', and recalls a plate in the *Director* (1st Edition, Plate XXXII). This bedstead, probably made by Chippendale for the fourth Duke of Beaufort, was formerly in a room 'finished and furnished very elegantly in the Chinese manner'. The bedstead was provided with curtains of Chinese silk or chintz, the disappearance of the original hangings somewhat detracting from its present appearance. The painted or 'japanned' furniture from David Garrick's bedroom at his Hampton villa again formed part of a consistent scheme of decoration. The room had a Chinese wallpaper, while the bed still retains its Indian cotton hangings, presented by some merchants of Calcutta to the actor's wife. It may be assumed that the contents of this room were supplied by Chippendale, for his firm furnished Garrick's house in the Adelphi in a similar style, and the Museum possesses the original accounts for this transaction. Among the comparatively few objects which correspond with published designs are an organ case (Fig. 111) and set of chairs (Fig. 49), of which the backs have their exact counterpart in the *Director* (1st Edition, Plate XII), while the 'ribband-back' examples (Fig. 69) are renderings of a celebrated design in which the author took a special pride.

Owing to the great reputation of his book, Chippendale's name overshadows that of his contemporaries, and he was formerly held responsible for all the best mahogany furniture of this period, mostly the work of other hands. His genius as a craftsman, or at least, as the organizer of a highly successful business, is proved by the contents of such houses as Harewood and Nostell Priory, where his productions are authenticated by receipted bills. But it is significant that, though the period of his activity saw large orders given for furnishing the Royal palaces, Chippendale's name does not occur in the accounts of the Lord Chamberlain's Department. Prominent among the craftsmen employed by the Crown were John Bradburn, Benjamin Goodison, and the partners William Vile and John Cobb. A mahogany bureau-cabinet, supplied by Vile and still at Buckingham Palace, has all the characteristics of the so-called 'Chippendale style' and is of a quality unsurpassed by that famous maker. In other pieces Vile's personal taste is more clearly apparent. He favoured wreaths clasped with acanthus and pendants of fruit and flowers; the quality of his productions is of the highest order, and as an exponent of the rococo style, pride of place must henceforth be assigned to him. Vile is, as yet, unrepresented in the Collection.

The success of the *Director* led to the publication of other works, conceived in a spirit of rivalry. Of these, Ince and Mayhew's *Universal System of Household Furniture*, published in parts between 1759 and 1763, is the most important. Though the public are admonished to cultivate propriety and a 'peculiar neatness through the whole house', this advice is discounted by the extravagance of the designs in the Gothic and Chinese styles. The plates, which are made 'as easy as possible to the capacity of every workman' by the addition of profile mouldings, include a few varieties of furniture not illustrated in the *Director*, notably tea tables with tripod stands (*cf.* Figs. 18 and 19). William Ince appears to have been the dominant partner, signing the majority of the designs. On the trade label their partners announce that they sell 'French furniture' consigned from Paris, and the notes are printed in English and French, an indication that they hoped to secure a foreign market. In this aspiration they were not alone. Giles Grendey of Clerkenwell exported 'japanned' furniture, and the Museum possesses a couch, japanned red with gilt enrichments, which formed part of a set made early in the century by Grendey for a castle in Spain.

Furniture in the rococo style has been traced to the designs of several of Chippendale's contemporaries, such as Ince and Mayhew, Johnson (*see* Figs. 79 and 86), and Lock and Copeland, who, besides collaborating for the *Director*, published a number of independent works. Robert Manwaring specialized in designing chairs, and an example in the Museum (Fig. 54) recalls types shown in his book, *The Cabinet and Chair Makers Real Friend and Companion*. Attributions to individual makers, in the absence of bills, are hazardous, for pattern-books were widely circulated and supplied models to the trade. That the high standard of craftsmanship which distinguishes this period was not confined to the capital is proved by the knee-hole writing table (Fig. 37) which is inscribed in faded ink on the bottom of a drawer (the third to the left of the knee-hole), 'David Wright, Lancaster, Fecit, August 11, 1751'. This is one of the very rare instances so far recorded of an autograph inscription on a piece of English eighteenth-century furniture, and is of particular interest in view of Pennant's statement in 1772 that Lancaster is 'famous in having some very ingenious cabinet-makers settled here'. For at least a generation the furniture for the London branch of the well-known firm of Gillow had been manufactured in the town. Though mahogany was the usual material during the rococo phase of design, a large quantity of walnut furniture was produced down to the middle of the eighteenth century.*

The classical revival, with which the name of Robert Adam will always be associated, dates from the early years of George III's reign, and first attained definite expression in the homes of a few great magnates. In 1762 Adam produced his plans for providing the Duke of Northumberland with a suite of rooms at Syon 'entirely in the antique style'; and there, as in other houses, furniture formed an integral part of the general scheme. The style was free from any marked archaeological bias and was essentially eclectic, the repertory of ornament being drawn from the same sources as the contemporary mural decoration (*see supra*). Indeed, so consistent was the treatment that in houses equipped under Adam's supervision the same patterns and decorative motifs are frequently found on ceilings, carpets, and inlaid furniture. Among the details derived from classical sources – the 'Ancient works in the Baths and Villas of the Romans', in Sir John Soane's phrase – are the anthemion or honeysuckle ornament, so often used for ornamental borders, oval pateræ, medallions, and festoons of husks. Other prominent decorative ingredients are terminal figures, ram-headed capitals, vases, and urns. In wall furniture such as cabinets and bookcases, there was a return to the architectural pediments and entablatures of the Palladian school; but the proportions were more carefully studied and the mouldings more accurate. The furniture produced under Adam's supervision was of a ceremonial character suited to the 'parade of life'. A characteristic arrangement, which may be attributed to him, is the sideboard flanked by urn-surmounted pedestals. In houses designed by Adam, a group of this kind took the place of the isolated side-table hitherto employed for serving food. Torchères and tripods, painted or gilded, were also freely used in saloons and drawing-rooms to support vases or candelabra. A pair of such stands from 20 St James's Square, which was perhaps the finest of Adam's town houses, are in the Museum Collection (Fig. 87). The more delicate ornament is carved in pinewood and applied on a ground of mahogany; on the removal of modern paint and gilding, the original colour was revealed. These pedestals formed part of the furnishings of the Eating Room, the delicate blue and ivory-white matching the decoration of the walls. The interior decoration of Osterley Park House, carried out between 1761 and 1780, shows some of Adam's most felicitous designs (Figs. 5, 6 and 7).

Tapered and fluted supports, rectangular or of baluster shape, supplanted the cabriole leg as being more in harmony with the severe and simple lines of the new style. Many chairs of this time have oval-, heart-, or shield-shaped backs with an openwork splat, or symmetrically

---

* Throughout this period the furniture made for the governing class is divided by a wide gulf in the quality of the materials employed, excellence of carving and technical 'finish', from that supplied to ordinary citizens. Distinction of design deriving from a long-established tradition and the makers' innate appreciation of form is a more widely distributed attribute, and is often found in furniture of relatively mediocre craftsmanship.

arranged bars of tracery. Upholstered chairs closely resembled the contemporary French models, and were covered with tapestry, damask, or leather (needlework was no longer fashionable), the woodwork being gilt or japanned.

Despite the force of Adam's example, 'the electric power of this revolution in art' (which incidentally was inaugurated before the parallel development in France) did not become manifest immediately. In the third edition of Chippendale's *Director* (1762) the rococo style still predominates, and there is no trace of classical influence. Yet, before his death (1779) Chippendale had assimilated the new ideals and, in association with Adam, produced furniture of extraordinary distinction. The work done at Harewood House between 1772 and 1775 'stands out among the few masterpieces of English furniture, comparable in technical brilliance with the finest achievements of the French cabinet-makers of the eighteenth century'; and henceforward Chippendale must rank as the supreme exponent of the neo-classical style, in contrast to the former conception of his achievement. In some of the most notable of these productions the art of marquetry is revived, and attains a technical excellence hitherto unparalleled. A variety of new exotic woods, stained and shaded, were employed with remarkable decorative effect, while satinwood was used by Chippendale as early as 1770. Several good specimens of this style of marquetry are in the Collection, notably a commode by John Cobb, a cabinet designed by Robert Adam for the Duchess of Manchester, and a small, fitted dressing-table of elegant design (Figs. 130, 144 and 30). Lacquered, or japanned, decoration was also restored to favour, especially for bedrooms, and Oriental panels were sometimes cut up to form commodes. There are two excellent examples at Osterley, one with carved wood details gilded to simulate ormolu (Fig. 128). Many of these costly pieces of inlaid or japanned furniture have finely chased ormolu mounts, the English production of such wares being stimulated by the establishment of Mathew Boulton's factory at Soho, near Birmingham, where he is said to have kept thirty-five chasers at work.

The degree of Adam's responsibility must not be exaggerated: others co-operated with him in effecting the change. The Museum possesses a large portfolio of designs for furniture 'made and for the most part executed during an extensive practice of many years in the first line of his profession by John Linnell, upholsterer, carver, and cabinetmaker'. This portfolio contains designs for a large variety of furniture, including chairs, settees, state beds, commodes, mirrors, and picture frames. They range from the rococo and Chinese to an original interpretation of the classical style. The notes show that Linnell (died 1799) was employed in a number of great houses, and was making furniture for Kedleston before Sir Nathaniel Curzon became Lord Scarsdale in 1761. He has now emerged as one of the most prominent makers of the period, and several fine examples have been traced to his designs. A similar ability to vary his style was shown by Lock, who, after being associated with the plates for Chippendale's *Director*, designed with considerable success in the classical manner. Another maker of high standing, now almost forgotten, was William France, who was employed by the first Lord Mansfield at Kenwood and Bloomsbury Square between 1768 and 1770, in association with Chippendale and Adam. France supplied most of the furniture to Kenwood, including large gilt pier glasses, which still remain in the house, and a mahogany reading-table now in the Museum (Fig. 20). Nor was Adam the only fashionable architect concerned in the production of furniture. In the Department of Engravings will be found designs for mirrors and candelabra by James Paine (1725–89), the builder of Brocket Hall; while there is evidence that Sir William Chambers, James Wyatt, and 'Athenian' Stuart also gave some attention to this subject.

The principles demonstrated by this group are found adapted to the use of cabinet-makers in the trade publications of the late eighteenth century. In Hepplewhite's *Guide* (1788), the neo-classic style, associated with Adam, is modified and skilfully translated into vernacular terms. The declared aim was 'to unite elegance and utility, and blend the useful with the agreeable'. Though the designs vary in merit, they show that from the diffusion of classical ideals a manner of furnishing, simple, rational, and elegant had resulted. Many of the objects illustrated were to be made in satin-wood, inlaid with various woods; while for other designs japanned (*i.e.* painted) decoration is recommended, 'a fashion that has arisen within these last few years'.*

The notes state that one of the chairs 'has been executed with good effect for the Prince of Wales', and it is possible that Hepplewhite's firm first popularized the familiar three feathers as an ornament. The *Guide* disowns originality and claims to have followed 'the latest or most prevailing fashion' in preference to mere novelty. Thus, the style represented is not so much the creation of any one individual as an expression of collective tendencies; indeed, it is doubtful if George Hepplewhite was personally responsible. No bills from the firm are known, nor can any furniture be definitely assigned to it. Designs scarcely distinguishable from those of the *Guide* are to be found in the *London Cabinetmakers' Book of Prices* (1788). A few plates in that catalogue are signed 'Hepplewhite', but the majority are by Thomas Shearer, who also incorporated them in his *Designs for Household Furniture*. They include bureaux, bookcases, and sideboards, while he seems to have specialized in dressing-tables and washing-stands, of which the fittings are extremely ingenious.

A large number of craftsmen at this period are identified by bills, or by pieces of furniture bearing their trade labels. George Seddon, a cabinet-maker and upholsterer was established from about the middle of the century at 150 Aldersgate Street, 'a house with six wings'. In 1768 the *Annual Register* records the destruction by fire of London House, 'now occupied by Mr Seddon, one of the most eminent of cabinet-makers of London. The damage is computed at £20,000'. An inventory of the firm's stock in 1789 shows it to have been worth nearly six times the amount of their loss. From the diary of a German lady who visited the establishment in 1788, we obtain an exceptionally full description of this Georgian cabinet-maker's business.† Four hundred journeymen were employed, and the staff included upholsterers, carvers, gilders, mirror-makers, workers in ormolu, and locksmiths. In the showrooms were chairs, stools, and sofas 'made of all varieties of wood'; while the patterns for other varieties of furniture ranged 'from the simplest to the most elegant'. Seddon was 'for ever creating new forms', which implies that he was not only a maker but also a designer. Despite the vast scale of this undertaking, very few of the firm's productions have been identified. The painted chair (Fig. 62) closely resembles those in a large set which are authenticated by one of their bills. Under the name of Seddon and Sons, the firm was still

---

* Most of the japanned decoration of this time is merely varnished paint, the varnishes composed of gum, lac and other constituents on a prepared ground being no longer employed.

† *Tagebuch einer Reise durch Holland und England von der Verfasserin von Rosaliens Briefe*, Offenbach, 1788 (Marie Sophie von la Roche). *Sophie in London* (1788), translated from the German by Clare Williams, 1933, pp. 173–75.

prominent early in the nineteenth century, when it received large payments for the furnishings and decoration of Windsor Castle. George Seddon died in 1801 and a portrait of him in old age has been given to the Museum by a direct descendant.

The most important trade publication of the last half of the eighteenth century is Thomas Sheraton's *Drawing Book*, a work so ambitious and comprehensive that it has caused the author's name to be associated with most of the furniture produced in England between 1790 and 1800. Yet this classification is misleading. There is no reason to suppose that Sheraton, who was trained as a 'journeyman cabinetmaker', ever possessed a cabinetmaker's business of his own, or made any considerable quantity of furniture. His professed intention was 'to exhibit the present taste', and that some of the designs represent models already in use is suggested by various remarks in the Introduction. But Sheraton's imagination and technical knowledge were responsible for many improvements and modifications. Though it is possible to regard the designs in the *Drawing Book* merely as a representative collection of the types in vogue, if they are compared with the illustrations in Hepplewhite's *Guide*, published only three years earlier, it will be seen that the style has been largely transformed in the interval. For this result much of the credit must be given to Sheraton. That his book exerted a powerful influence is suggested by the fact that nearly six hundred and fifty cabinetmakers from all parts of England subscribed for it. While elegance and refinement are the chief characteristics in the designs of this period, practical cabinet-making, called by Sheraton 'one of the leading mechanical professions in every polite nation in Europe', reached the zenith of excellence. This technical mastery is particularly noticeable in such matters as carcase construction, dovetailing, and the running of delicate mouldings. The finest furniture of the late eighteenth century was made of satin-wood, often combined with a variety of costly veneers. Some admirable examples of this kind are included in the Museum collection, the inlaid satin-wood bookcase (Fig. 146) being worthy of special notice. There was also a large output of furniture made in soft wood and painted to accord with the coloured walls and soft-toned hangings of contemporary rooms. Such japanned furniture was essentially decorative, and some of the more important specimens are painted with figure subjects and mythological scenes, after the designs of Angelica Kauffmann, Zucchi, or Cipriani. For chairs, rectilinear shapes were coming into favour. Lattice-work or vertical moulded bars are characteristic designs for the backs, while the legs are often turned and the framework fluted.

Until the death of Adam in 1792, the influence of the Adam style was still paramount on furniture; though his designs were freely adapted by cabinetmakers, their classical origin was obscured in the pursuit of luxury and feminine grace. The modified version of the French *Directoire* style, which became current in England at the end of the eighteenth century, covered the whole field of decoration and furniture. In its later phases it was carried out with rigid consistency, and was animated by a doctrinaire, archaeological spirit. The aim was to reproduce the exact forms of antiquity where precedents existed, as for couches, chairs, and candelabra; and for objects unknown in the ancient world, the great majority, to provide designs which should be fully consonant in character. Thus, by a free use of symbolism and ornament, often exploited in the most incongruous positions, every variety of domestic furniture was made to conform to the prevailing ideals. Figuring prominently in these designs are archaic lions (Fig. 34), winged sphinxes, hocked animal legs (Fig. 92),

15

and emblems such as the 'fulmen of Jupiter'. These were said to be drawn from 'the best antique examples' of three civilizations – the Roman, the Greek, and the Egyptian; but during the last phase of this so-called Regency style, 'Grecian severity' became the ideal. The inordinate use of symbolism, of which the significance was naïvely expounded in contemporary pattern-books, is characteristic of the desire to gratify the insatiable demand for novelties at all cost. Classical prototypes were diligently studied by the more erudite designers, and many of the chairs of this time, with their wide top rails and sweeping curves, approximate very closely to the Greek *klismos* found represented in vase paintings and Athenian reliefs.

In the furniture he designed for Carlton House and Southill, Bedfordshire, about 1800, Henry Holland finely interpreted 'the beautiful spirit of antiquity'; but to render the letter also was the avowed aim of the more ardent enthusiasts. The designs of Thomas Hope, whose *Household Furniture and Interior Decoration* (1807) was 'a consistent archaeological fantasy', show the style disciplined by scholarship and a sense of fitness. In the preface it is claimed that the chief merit of the furniture illustrated 'consists in the chastity and play of its contours'; while breadth and repose of surface, distinctness and contrast of outline, and the opposition of plain and enriched parts 'are calculated to afford the eye the most lively, most permanent, and most unfading enjoyment' – an apt summary of the attributes of the style at its best. Its wilder extravagances are represented in George Smith's work, *Household Furniture* (1808), and Sheraton's incomplete *Cabinet-maker's Encyclopaedia* (1805). A comparison of kindred objects, one in the neo-classic, the other in the Regency style, will tell us more than any description of the contrast between them in spirit and outlook (*cf.* Figs. 91 and 92).

At this period it was held that 'mahogany, when used in houses of consequence, should be confined to the Parlor and Bedchamber Floors', while satin-wood, rose-wood, and tulip-wood, were considered appropriate to boudoirs and drawing-rooms. Much of the carved ornament was bronzed, or gilt, and metal inlays and appliques were freely used (Fig. 149). The fondness for striking contrasts of colour, characteristic of the early nineteenth century, is well shown in the secretaire veneered with zebra-wood and mounted with bronze terminals in the Egyptian style (Fig. 150). The couch, part of a gilt set made by the firm of Gillow in 1805 (Fig. 72), is another characteristic object, a free adaptation of the type associated with David's portrait of Madame Recamier. A library table with lion supports, and a monopodium from one of Hope's designs (Figs. 34, 35) represent the style in its more rational form, and show that masculine dignity and monumental character were achieved by its abler exponents.

The archaeological character of some of this furniture is apt to give a rather unfavourable impression of contemporary taste, but we should remember that it was designed in relation to a carefully considered decorative scheme, and cannot be fairly judged in isolation. Moreover, the Regency was the last consistent and recognizable style before all standards of traditional design were abandoned. The finest examples of this later classical revival show no sign of the rapidly approaching decadence and go far to excuse the wilder aberrations.

LIST OF ILLUSTRATIONS

17 SIDE-TABLE. Carved mahogany with marble (*porto-venere*) top. *About* 1750. H. 2 ft. 9½ in., L. 4 ft. 5½ in. Percival Griffiths Collection. *Given by the N.A.C.F.* (w.35–1938)

18 TABLE on tripod stand. Carved mahogany. Mid 18th century. H. 2 ft. 6 in., w. 2 ft. 8 in. *Given by Mr F. H. Reed* (w.66–1953)

19 TABLE on tripod stand ('Claw Table'). Carved mahogany. From Foster's Court Farm, near Gloucester. H. 2 ft. 4 in., DIAM. 2 ft. 7 in. *About* 1760 (w.53–1928)

20 READING-TABLE. Carved mahogany. Made in 1770 by William France, for the Library at Kenwood House, Hampstead, built by Robert Adam for the first Lord Mansfield. H. 2 ft. 6 in., TOP 2 ft. 2 in. square (w.202–1923)

21 TEA-TABLE. Carved mahogany. *About* 1760. H. 2 ft. 4½ in., L. 2 ft. 7½ in. Percival D. Griffiths Collection. *Given by the N.A.C.F.* (w.34–1938)

22 CARD-TABLE. Carved mahogany. *About* 1760. H. 2 ft. 4 in., open 3 ft. square. *Browett Gift* (w.57–1937)

23 CARD-TABLE. Mahogany. *About* 1765–70. H. 2 ft. 4½ in., w. 2 ft. 11½ in. *Bequeathed by the late F. D. Brown* (w.1–1927)

24 TEA-TABLE. Mahogany, with fretwork decoration in the 'Chinese' taste. Mid 18th century. H. 2 ft. 4 in., L. 2 ft. 11½ in., w. 1½ in. *Given by the Misses Mary and Zielia Marsham* (w.35–1950)

25 BREAKFAST-TABLE. Mahogany (Chippendale's *Director*, 1754, Pl. xxxiii). H. 2 ft. 4 in., w. 2 ft. 5½ in. *Florence Bequest* (w.82–1917)

26 TOP OF NO. 27. Decoration painted on metal plates

27 SIDE-TABLE. Wood, painted and gilt; the top decorated in the style of Angelica Kauffmann. *About* 1790. H. 2 ft. 8 in., w. 3 ft. 10 in. (349A–1871)

28 TOP OF NO. 29

29 SIDE-TABLE. Painted pinewood. On the top an applied oval of parchment painted in grisaille and inscribed *Lucy Ussher Fecit:* Irish. *About* 1790. H. 3 ft., L. 3 ft. 11 in. (w.10–1920)

30 DRESSING-TABLE. Mahogany, with marquetry of various woods. *About* 1775. H. 2 ft. 4 in., L. 2 ft. 5¾ in. Mulliner Collection. *Given by Mrs H. H. Mulliner* (w.89–1924)

31 WRITING-TABLE. Satinwood, inlaid with various woods. *About* 1790. H. 2 ft. 9 in., w. 2 ft. *Given by Mr H. A. Bowler* (w.40–1922)

32 WORK-TABLE. Satinwood, with mahogany stringing lines. Fitted with writing drawer. *About* 1790. H. 2 ft. 6 in., w. 1 ft. 8 in. *Lloyd Bequest* (w.59–1927)

33 FOLDING-TABLE. ('Pembroke' table). Mahogany and inlaid satinwood. *About* 1790. H. 2 ft. 4½ in., w. 2 ft. 6 in. *Bequeathed by Mrs C. P. Holliday* (w.8–1935)

34 LIBRARY TABLE. Rosewood, with brass mounts. The top covered with leather, the lion terminal legs gilded. *About* 1810. H. 2 ft. 7 in., DIAM. 3 ft. 3½ in. (w.49–1946)

35 CIRCULAR TABLE (*monopodium*). Mahogany, inlaid with ebony and silver. Designed by Thomas Hope for his house, Deepdene, Surrey, and corresponding with Pl. xxxix in his *Household Furniture*, 1807. H. 2 ft. 5 in., DIAM. 3 ft. 6 in. (w.13–1936)

36 DRESSING-TABLE. Mahogany, inlaid with ebony. After a design, dated 1805, in George Smith's *Household Furniture*, 1808, Pl. lxxii. H. 2 ft. 4 in., L. 3 ft. 10 in. *From the Edward Knoblock Collection* (w.25–1946)

37 PEDESTAL WRITING-TABLE. Carved mahogany. Inscribed in ink on the bottom of a drawer: *David Wright Fecit Lancaster August 11, 1751.* H. 2 ft. 6½ in., w. 3 ft. 8½ in. *Murray Bequest* (w.8–1942)

38 BUREAU DRESSING TABLE. Carved mahogany with ormulu mounts, perhaps the work of a German immigré cabinet maker. Mid 18th century. H. 2 ft. 11 in. w. 5 ft. 1 in. *Purchased with the aid of a grant from the N.A.C.F. and a contribution from Messrs H. Blairman & Sons.* (w.4–1956)

39 LIBRARY-TABLE. Carved mahogany with gilt brass mounts. The lion masks resemble those on a library-table attributed to Chippendale at Badminton (see Ralph Edwards and Margaret Jourdain, *Georgian Cabinet-makers*, 1946. Fig. 76). *About* 1755–60. H. 2 ft. 7 in., w. 5 ft. 3 in. *Purchased with the aid of a grant from the N.A.C.F.* (w.56–1948)

40 LIBRARY-TABLE. Mahogany, with veneer of sabicu. Carved emblems of Architecture, Music: Comedy, Tragedy: Peace, War: Medicine, Letters. *About* 1810. H. 2 ft. 7 in., w. 8 ft. 0½ in. (w.28–1938)

41 DINING-TABLE IN TWO SECTIONS. Mahogany, with inlaid detail. *About* 1775. H. 2 ft. 5½ in., L. 7 ft. 2 in. (w.37–1929)

42 SIDEBOARD. Mahogany, inlaid with ebonized stringing lines. *About* 1795. H. 3 ft., w. 5 ft. 6 in. *Browett Gift* (w.47–1937)

43 SIDEBOARD. Mahogany, with satinwood stringing lines. *About* 1790. H. 2 ft. 2 in., w. 5 ft. 10 in. *Florence Bequest* (w.76–1917)

44 SIDEBOARD. Mahogany with carved lion-mask ornament. *About* 1800. H. 3 ft. 1 in. w. 7 ft.
(w.41–1950)

45 CHAIR. Beechwood, carved and gilt. Arms, granted in 1717, of Sir William Humphreys, Bart., Lord Mayor of London 1714–15. Contemporary Genoese velvet. H. 4 ft., w. 2 ft. 0½ in. (w.62–1935)

46 ARM-CHAIR. Walnut, with eagle terminals, upholstered in velvet. *About* 1725. H. 3 ft. 6 in., w. 2 ft. 9 in. *Given by the children of the late Sir George Donaldson* (w.38–1925)

47 LIBRARY READING-CHAIR. Carved mahogany upholstered in leather. Believed to have been in possession of the poet John Gay (1685–1732). *About* 1720. H. 2 ft. 9 in., w. 2 ft. 7 in.
(w.47–1948)

48 CHAIR. Carved mahogany. Crest of Eyre. One of a set of six. *About* 1740. H. 3 ft. 2½ in., w. 2 ft. 0½ in. *Douglas Eyre Gift* (w.32 to 32e–1922)

49 ARM-CHAIR. Carved mahogany. Seat upholstered in gros-point needlework of silk and wools. One of a set. Splat corresponds with Chippendale's *Director*, 1754, Pl. xii. H. 3 ft. 1¾ in., w. 2 ft. 2½ in. *Macquoid Gift* (w.46–1925)

50 ARM-CHAIR. Carved mahogany, upholstered with contemporary tent-stitch of silk and wools. *En suite* with the stool no. 66. H. 3 ft. 11 in. w. 2 ft. 10 in. *Given by Brigadier W. E. Clarke, C.M.G., D.S.O., through the N.A.C.F.* (w.16–1956)

51 ARM-CHAIR. Carved mahogany, with damask upholstery. Based on a design for a 'French chair' in Chippendale's *Director*, 3rd edition, 1762, Pl. xxii. H. 3 ft. 6½ in., w. 2 ft. 5 in. *Given by Brigadier W. E. Clark, C.M.G., D.S.O. through the N.A.C.F.*
(w.47–1946)

52 ARM-CHAIR. Carved mahogany, with arms, painted and gilt. Chair of the President of Lyon's Inn, an Inn of Chancery. *About* 1760. H. 4 ft. 2 in., w. 2 ft. 9 in. (w.63–1911)

53 ARM-CHAIR. Beech, veneered with parquetry of walnut and sycamore. In the 'Chinese' style. *About* 1760–70. H. 2 ft. 8 in., w. 1 ft. 9½ in. *Given by Mr Randolph Berens* (884–1901)

54 CHAIR. Carved mahogany. One of a pair. Style of Robert Manwaring. *About* 1770. H. 3 ft. 3 in., w. 2 ft. *Given by Mr Frank Green* (w.9–1932)

55 CHAIR. Carved mahogany, with 'ladder' back. *About* 1775. H. 3 ft. 1½ in., w. 2 ft. 0½ in. *Browett Gift* (w.72–1937)

56 ARM-CHAIR. Carved mahogany. *About* 1775. H. 3 ft. w. 2 ft. 0¾ in. *Given by Mr Edward Dent* (w.21–1922)

57 ARM-CHAIR. Mahogany veneered with rosewood, satinwood and other woods and enriched with gilt brass mounts. One of a set made for the Library at Osterley Park, probably by John Linnell. *About* 1770. H. 2 ft. 11½ in., w. 2 ft. 0½ in., D. 1 ft. 9½ in.

58 ARM-CHAIR. Carved and gilt beechwood. Part of a set made, probably by Samuel Norman, from a design, dated 1764, by Robert Adam, for Sir Lawrence Dundas, of Moor Park, Hertfordshire, and No. 19 Arlington Street. H. 3 ft. 6 in., w. 2 ft. 6½ in. (w.1–1937)

59 ARM-CHAIR. Carved mahogany. Style of Sheraton. *About* 1790. H. 2 ft. 11 in., w. 1 ft. 10½ in.
(w.86–1929)

60 ARM-CHAIR. Mahogany. with painted decoration. *About* 1785. H. 3 ft. 2 in., w. 1 ft. 11 in.
(w.52–1946)

61 ARM-CHAIR (one of a pair). Beechwood with carved and painted decoration. From Woodhall Park, Hertfordshire. Probably designed about 1778 by Thomas Leverton. H. 3 ft. 2½ in., w. 2 ft. 1¼ in. (w.18–1931)

62 ARM-CHAIR. Satinwood, with painted decoration. Probably by Seddon & Sons and Shackleton. *About* 1790. H. 3 ft. 0½ in., w. 1 ft. 8½ in. *Given by Mrs Simon Green* (w.59–1936)

63 ARM-CHAIR. Carved mahogany. *About* 1785–90. H. 2 ft. 11 in., w. 2 ft. 0½ in. *Given by Mr Donald Gunn* (w.64–1930)

64 ARM-CHAIR. Soft wood, with carved, japanned and gilt gesso decoration, in the 'Grecian' taste. *About* 1810. H. 2 ft. 10¾ in., w. 2 ft. 0 in. (w.5–1939)

65 STOOL. One of a pair in walnut, upholstered in Italian seventeenth-century brocade. *About* 1720. H. 1 ft. 7¾ in., w. 1 ft. 8 in. *Croft Lyons Bequest* (w.55–1926)

66 STOOL. Carved mahogany, with dolphin legs, *en suite* with the arm-chair (no. 50). Compare Chippendale's *Director*, 1754, Pl. xx (2). Mid 18th century. H. 1 ft. 6½ in., L. 2 ft. 1½ in. (w.39–1946)

67 SETTEE. Walnut, upholstered in Soho tapestry. From Glemham Hall, Suffolk. Early eighteenth century. H. 3 ft. 6 in., L. 5 ft. 1 in. (w.29–1947)

68 SETTEE. Soft wood, carved, painted and gilt; upholstery in crimson velvet. Style of William Kent. *About* 1735. L. 5 ft. 6 in., H. 3 ft. 3½ in. *Murray Bequest* (w.48–1934)

69 SETTEE. Carved mahogany. Compare Chippendale's *Director*, 1754, Pl. xvi ('Ribband Back' chairs). *About* 1755. *Clarke Bequest* (w.64–1935)

70 SETTEE. Carved mahogany, in the 'Chinese' style. From Ingress Abbey, Kent. *About* 1748. H. 3 ft. 2½ in., w. 5 ft. 4½ in. *Bryan Bequest*
(w.7–1946)

71 SETTEE. Japanned wood, caned. H. 3 ft. 1 in., w. 5 ft. *About* 1790 (w.41–1931)

72 SETTEE. Carved and gilt beechwood. From a set made by Gillows, London, in 1805, for Kimmel Park, Co. Denbigh. *Heaton Tabb Gift.* H. 2 ft. 8½ in., w. 6 ft. 8 in. (w.38–1930)

73 MIRROR. Pinewood frame, carved and gilt. Probably designed by William Kent, for Frederick, Prince of Wales, and made by Benjamin Goodison. H. 5 ft. 10 in., w. 2 ft. 5 in. *Stern Gift. About* 1740.
(w.86–1911)

74 MIRROR. Carved and gilt gesso. The original water gilding preserved by coats of paint recently removed. *About* 1730. H. 6 ft. 2 in., w. 3 ft. 6½ in.
(w.46–1948)

75 MIRROR, with barometer and thermometer. Pine-wood frame, carved and gilt. *About* 1730. H. 7 ft. 5½ in., w. 3 ft. 10⅛ in. (w.44–1927)

76 MIRROR. Pinewood frame with burr-walnut veneer and gilt gesso detail. *About* 1730. H. 3 ft. 10½ in., w. 2 ft. 2 in. (w.16–1927)

77 MIRROR. Pinewood frame with carved and gilt gesso decoration. *About* 1725. H. 3 ft. 10½ in., w. 2 ft. 2 in. (w.29–1927)

78 MIRROR. Carved pinewood, veneered with mahogany and partly gilt. Mid 18th century. H. 4 ft. 4 in., w. 2 ft. 3⅜ in. (w.85–1910)

79 CHIMNEY GLASS. Carved and gilt wood frame. Ganymede bearing the Lightning. Based on a design by Thomas Johnson. *About* 1760. H. 4 ft. 2 in., w. 4 ft. 4 in. (w.36–1947)

80 CHIMNEY GLASS. Carved and gilt wood frame. Probably designed for a room in the 'Chinese' taste. *About* 1750–60. H. 4 ft., w. 4 ft. 6 in. (w.33–1947)

81 MIRROR. One of a pair. Pinewood frame with carved and gilt gesso decoration. Probably by Thomas Chippendale. *About* 1760. H. 7 ft., w. 4 ft. 6 in. *From the Bernal Collection.* (2388–1855)

82 CHIMNEY GLASS. Pinewood, carved and gilt. From Bradbourne, Kent. *About* 1774. H. 6 ft. 10 in., w. 6 ft. 5 in. (w.66–1938)

83 MIRROR. Pinewood frame, carved and gilt, with convex glass. *About* 1800. H. 8 ft. 4 in., w. 3 ft. 6 in. (w.85–1926)

84 MIRROR. Carved and gilt pinewood frame. *About* 1810. H. 3 ft. 7½ in., w. 2 ft. 2 in.
(w.60–1937)

85 PEDESTAL (one of a pair). Moulded terra-cotta, painted. *About* 1730. H. 3 ft. 9⅜ in., w. 8 in.
(w.5 and A.–1946)

86 CANDLESTAND. Carved pinewood, one of a set of four corresponding closely with a design, dated 1756, by Thomas Johnson (*One Hundred and Fifty New Designs*, Pl. 13) which was adapted by Thomas Chippendale (*Gentleman's and Cabinet Maker's Director*, 1762, Pl. CXLV). *From Hagley Park, Worcestershire.* H. 5 ft. 2½ in., w. 1 ft. 10 in.
(w.9–1950)

87 CANDLESTAND. Carved mahogany and pinewood, painted (original decoration in blue and ivory white lately exposed). From the Eating-Room, 20 St James's Square. Designed by Robert Adam for Sir Watkin Williams-Wynn. 1771–4. H. 4 ft., side of bases, 1 ft. 10½ in. (w.36 and A.–1946)

88 PEDESTAL (one of a pair). Wood, carved, painted and gilt. From a set made, probably by Samuel Norman, to a design by Robert Adam, for Sir Lawrence Dundas of No. 19 Arlington Street and Moor Park, Hertfordshire. *About* 1765. H. 4 ft. 6 in., side of base 10½ in. *N.A.C.F.* (w.24–1934)

89 CANDLESTAND (one of a pair). Carved and gilt wood. *About* 1770. H. 5 ft. 7¾ in., DIAM. 1 ft. 9 in. (w.72 and A.–1923)

90 CANDLESTAND. Pinewood, carved and gilt. *About* 1770. H. 4 ft. 6½ in. (w.37–1937)

91 SIDEBOARD PEDESTAL (one of a pair). Carved mahogany. H. 5 ft. 4 in., w. 1 ft. 8 in. *About* 1770. *Given by Mr John A. Tulk*
(w.38 and A.–1934)

92 STAND (one of a pair). Carved mahogany. Resembling a design by Thomas Hope (*Household Furniture*, 1807, Pl. ii). H. 2 ft. 9 in.
(w.35 and A.–1946)

93 CHANDELIER. Carved and gilt wood. *About* 1725. From Hamilton Palace. H. 3 ft. 3 in., DIAM. 2 ft. 9 in. (416–1882)

94 BRACKET. Carved pinewood (gilding modern). Mask of Venus. *About* 1760. From Langley Park, Norwich. H. 2 ft. 2 in., w. 1 ft. 9 in. (w.50–1946)

95 BRACKET. Carved pinewood (gilding modern). Mask of Bacchus. Corresponding with a design, dated 1760 (Chippendale's *Director*, 1762, Pl. clxi, 6), for 'Brackets for Bustos'. From Langley Park, Norwich (w.50A.–1946)

96 MIRROR WITH CANDLE BRANCHES. Carved and gilt pinewood, designed by Robert Adam for the Gallery at Osterley Park. *About* 1770. H. 7 ft. 6 in., w. 4 ft. 9 in.

97 WALL-LANTERN. Carved mahogany, one of a pair. The back of looking glass. English. *About* 1740. H. 2 ft. 8 in., w. 1 ft. 4 in. *Given by Brigadier W. E. Clark,* C.M.G., D.S.O. (w.63–1950)

98 CANDELABRUM (one of a pair). Fluor-spar ('Blue John') with ormolu mounts. Made by Matthew Boulton (*b.* 1728, *d.* 1809) for Sir Lawrence Dundas, Moor Park, Herts. *About* 1765. H. 2 ft. 8½ in. *N.A.C.F.* (w.23 and A.–1934)

99 STAND ('Tea Kettle Stand'). Mahogany. Similar to Chippendale's *Director*, 1762, Pl. lv. H. 1 ft. 11 in., w. 11½ in. (213–1885)

100 ARMILLARY SPHERE. Carved Mahogany, with celestial sphere in brass. *About* 1750. H. 3 ft. 2½ in., DIAM. 1 ft. 9 in. Percival Griffiths Collection. *Given by the N.A.C.F.* (w.36–1938)

101 TERRESTRIAL GLOBE. On mahogany stand. One of a pair by W. and T. M. Bardin. Globe dated 1843. Stand *about* 1800. DIAM. of globe, 1 ft. 6 in., H. of stand, 1 ft. 11¾ in. *Given by Mr Murray Marks* (w.52–1916)

102 WASHSTAND. Carved and turned mahogany. *About* 1760. H. 2 ft. 8 in., w. 1 ft. 4½ in. (w.50–1910)

103 TEAPOY. Rosewood, with parquetry of various woods (Tunbridge Ware). Brass feet. H. 2 ft. 7 in., w. 1 ft. 5½ in. *About* 1820. *F. L. Lucas Bequest* (w.5–1931)

104 URN-TABLE. Satinwood, with painted decoration. Mark: *M. Gregson Liverpool* 1790, for Matthew Gregson (*b.* 1749, *d.* 1824), upholsterer and antiquary. H. 2 ft. 4½ in., w. 1 ft. 2½ in. *Bequeathed by Lady Isabella D. Wilson* (w.45–1935)

105 KNIFE-CASE. Satinwood, with painted decoration. *About* 1780. H. 2 ft. 5½ in., DIAM. 1 ft. 1½ in. (w.28–1912)

106 POLE-SCREEN. Carved mahogany, with petit-point embroidery. *About* 1760. H. 6 ft. 0½ in., w. 2 ft. 3½ in. (w.1–1928)

107 SCREEN. Wood frame, carved and gilt, with petit-point embroidery. Resembles Chippendale's designs for 'Horse Fire-Screens' (*Director*, 1754, Pl. cxxvii). H. 3 ft. 2 in., w. 2 ft. *Murray Bequest* (w.2–1933)

108 POLE-SCREEN. Mahogany, with panel of petit-point embroidery. *About* 1760. H. 2 ft. 8 in., w. 1 ft. 9 in. *Croft Lyons Bequest* (w.60–1926)

109 PAIR OF KNIFE-BOXES. Yew veneer, with silver mounts. *About* 1770. H. (shut) 1 ft. 3½ in., w. 10¼ in. (w.90 and A.–1926)

110 TEA-CADDIES. Inlaid: (*a*) harewood; (*b*) satinwood; (*c*) walnut; stamped: *Gillows Lancaster. About* 1790. H. (*a*) 4⅝ in., H. (*b*) 5 in., (*c*) 4⅜ in. (w.98, 108, 101–1919)

111 ORGAN-CASE. Carved mahogany. Based on a design dated 1760 (Chippendale's *Director*, 1762, Pl. cv). From Polebarn House, Trowbridge. *Bequeathed by the late J. M. Courage.* H. 11 ft. 4 in., w. 6 ft. 6 in. (w.37–1931)

112 HANGING CLOCK. Mahogany case with carved and gilt decoration applied. *About* 1760. H. 5 ft. 10 in., w. 2 ft. 5 in. *Given by Lord Riddell* (w.4–1935)

113 CLOCK ('Act of Parliament' clock) in case with japanned decoration. Inscribed *Humphrey Sellon, Southwark.* H. 5 ft. 4 in., w. 2 ft. 7 in. *About* 1750 (w.51–1927)

114 LONG-CASE CLOCK. Pinewood case with decoration carved, japanned and silvered. Movement by Markwick, the younger. *About* 1725. H. 9 ft. 4 in., w. 2 ft. 0½ in. *Bryan Bequest* (w.49–1935)

115 LONG-CASE CLOCK. Case, with walnut veneer and marquetry of various woods. Movement by William Halstead, London. *About* 1720. H. 9 ft. 7½ in., w. 1 ft. 10½ in. *Bequeathed by Mrs A. Anderson* (w.24–1938)

116 LONG-CASE CLOCK. Oak, with carved, japanned and silvered decoration. Movement by Thomas Windmills, of St Martin's-le-Grand. *About* 1725. H. 8 ft. 8 in., w. 1 ft. 10½ in. *Hudson Bequest* (w.17–1937)

117 LONG-CASE CLOCK. Oak, with japanned decoration. Movement by John Ellicott. *About* 1750. H. 7 ft. 3 in., w. 1 ft. 8 in. *Winstanley Bequest* (w.20–1946)

118 LONG-CASE CLOCK. Case, veneered with figured walnut. Movement by Francis Jullion. *About* 1780. H. 7 ft. 10 in., w. 1 ft. 9 in. *Winstanley Bequest* (w.21–1946)

119 LONG-CASE CLOCK. Mahogany, with gilt-brass mounts. Movement by Davison/Ecclesham. *About* 1775. H. 7 ft. 11½ in., w. 2 ft. *Browett Gift* (w.50–1937)

120 LONG-CASE CLOCK. Carved mahogany case with brass face partly silvered. Movement by William Barker, Wigan. *About* 1780. H. 7 ft. 9 in., w. 1 ft. 9½ in. (w.81–1910)

121 LONG-CASE CLOCK. Mahogany case inlaid with satinwood. Movement by Edward Shepley, Manchester. *About* 1780. H. 7 ft. 7 in., w. 2 ft. 2 in. *Given by Mr Emile S. Mond* (w.12–1911)

122 BAROMETER AND THERMOMETER. Carved mahogany case. Instruments by James Ayscough, Great Golden Spectacles, Ludgate Street. *About* 1755. H. 3 ft. 6 in., w. 7 in. *Buckston Browne Gift* (w.27–1926)

123 BRACKET CLOCK in case, with japanned decoration. By James Markwick, the younger. *About* 1730. H. 1 ft. 6 in., w. 10½ in. *Johnson Bequest* (w.7–1944)

124 BAROMETER AND THERMOMETER. Mahogany case. Instruments by John Russell, of Falkirk, watchmaker to George, Prince of Wales. *About* 1800. H. 4 ft., w. 1 ft. 1 in. (w.18–1936)

125 COMMODE CHEST. Carved mahogany. *About* 1760. H. 2 ft. 9 in., w. 3 ft. 6 in. (w.133–1919)

126 DRESSING COMMODE. Mahogany, inlaid with satinwood and ebonized wood. *About* 1775. H. 2 ft. 9 in., w. 3 ft. 8½ in. *Browett Gift* (w.55–1937)

127 COMMODE. Oak, with japanned decoration. *About* 1775. H. 2 ft. 10½ in., w. 3 ft. 5⅞ in. (w.61–1931)

128 COMMODE. Veneered with black and gold Chinese lacquer, the ram's-head pilasters of carved wood gilded to simulate ormolu. Probably made from a design by Robert Adam. From the State Bedchamber, Osterley Park. *About* 1775. H. 2 ft. 11 in., L. 5 ft. 3 in., D. 1 ft. 11½ in.

129 TOP OF NO. 130

130 COMMODE. Mahogany, with marquetry of various woods and ormolu mounts. Made by John Cobb of 72 St Martin's Lane, upholsterer to George III. *About* 1775. H. 2 ft. 10½ in., L. 3 ft. 8 in. (w.30–1937)

131 DRESSING TABLE. Mahogany, with kingwood veneer and marquetry of various woods. *About* 1775. H. 2 ft. 7 in., w. 4 ft. 1½ in. *Given by Mr Frank Partridge* (w.55–1928)

132 COMMODE. Harewood, with marquetry of various woods by William Moore of Dublin. *About* 1785. H. 2 ft. 10¾ in., w. 4 ft. 7¾ in. (w.56–1925)

133 COMMODE. Satinwood, with laburnum banding and marquetry of various woods. *About* 1775. H. 2 ft. 10 in., w. 2 ft. 5½ in. *From the Mulliner Collection. Given by Mrs H. H. Mulliner* (w.88–1924)

134 COMMODE. Satinwood, with bandings of rosewood and painted decoration. *About* 1790. H. 2 ft. 10 in., w. 3 ft. 6 in. (636–1870)

135 COMMODE (one of a pair). Satinwood, with painted decoration. *About* 1790. H. 2 ft. 11 in., w. 4 ft. 6 in. *Lloyd Bequest* (w.58 and A.–1927)

136 BUREAU-CABINET. Walnut, crossbanded and inlaid with box and holly, the eagle gilded. *About* 1720. H. 7 ft. 11 in., w. 3 ft. 4½ in. *Given by Mrs M. L. Sturrock* (w.11–1944)

137 BUREAU-CABINET. Carved mahogany. *About* 1750. H. 8 ft. 4 in., w. 3 ft. 7½ in. *Badcock Bequest* (w.37–1935)

138 SECRETARY. Mahogany with marquetry of tortoiseshell and inlay of engraved brass. Perhaps the work of an immigrant continental cabinet-maker. *About* 1720–30. H. 8 ft. 3 in., w. 3 ft. 1 in., D. 2 ft. 11 in. (w.37–1953)

139 CHINA-CABINET. Carved mahogany. Originally at Charlton House, Kent, and probably made for John Perceval, First Earl of Egmont. H. 6 ft. 11 in., w. 4 ft. 6½ in. *About* 1745. *From the Mulliner Collection. Murray Bequest* (w.53–1925)

140 BOOKCASE. Pinewood, carved and painted with gilt enrichments. Style of William Kent. *About* 1730. H. 7 ft. 1½ in., w. 5 ft. 7 in. (w.2–1923)

141 CABINET. Carved kingwood, with figures of Palladio, Fiammingo and Inigo Jones, the arms of Walpole, eagle-heads and plaques of ivory. Made for Horace Walpole in 1743. H. 5 ft., w. 3 ft (w.52–1925)

142 CABINET ON STAND. Carved mahogany with pagoda top, the finials of gilt metal, the cabinet Chinese, the front veneered with tortoiseshell and set with panels of carved ivory. Mid 18th century. H. 5 ft. 11½ in., w. 1 ft. 9 in. *Given by Mr F. H. Reed* (w.65–1953)

143 CHINA CABINET. On stand in 'Gothick' taste, carved mahogany. *About* 1760. H. 8 ft. 4 in., L. 4 ft. 0 in., D. 1 ft. 9½ in. (w.45–1953)

144 CABINET. Marquetry of satinwood, rosewood and other woods, and of marble intarsia panels, with mounts of gilt brass. The marble panels signed and dated *Baccio Cappelli fecit Anno 1709 Fiorenza*. This cabinet was designed by Robert Adam for Elizabeth, Duchess of Manchester, in 1771 to provide a setting for the eleven panels of marble intarsia. From Kimbolton Castle, Huntingdonshire. H. 6 ft. 2¼ in., w. 5 ft. 10 in. (w.43–1949)

145 CABINET. Mahogany, inlaid with satinwood. *About* 1775. H. 7 ft. 1 in., w. 3 ft. 8 in. *Bequeathed by Sir Herbert Mitchell,* K.C.V.O. (w.50–1936)

146 SECRETARY-BOOKCASE. Satinwood, with inlay of various woods, painted decoration. *About* 1790. H. 6 ft. 10 in., w. 4 ft. 4 in. *Given by Sir Claude Phillips* (w.121–1924)

147 HANGING CABINET. Mahogany, inlaid with brass. Ebonized metal and various woods. Crocodile, arrows and lyres, an allusion to Nelson's victory of the Nile (1797). H. 6 ft. 2½ in., w. 3 ft. 9½ in. *Murray Bequest* (w.63–1935)

148 SECRETARY. Carved satinwood. Drawer at side fitted for painting. *Given by Princess Mary, daughter of George III, to Helena Perceval in 1816.* H. 4 ft. 2 in., w. 2 ft. 7 in. (w.12–1931)

149 SECRETARY. Rosewood, with satinwood stringing and brass mounts. Made by John McLean & Son, 58 Upper Marylebone Street. *About* 1810. *Murray Bequest* (w.10–1944)

150 SECRETARY. Mahogany, veneered with zebrawood. Water colours of Clyde scenes, signed: *J. Baynes* 1808. H. 5 ft. 2½ in., w. 2 ft. 6¾ in. (w.15–1930)

151 CABINET. Satinwood with inlaid banding, painted detail and gilt brass mounts. *About* 1820. H. 4 ft. 2½ in., w. 2 ft. 5 in. *Given by Mr F. H. Reed* (w.64–1953)

152 WARDROBE. Carved mahogany. *About* 1750. H. 5 ft. 7 in., w. 4 ft. 1½ in. (w.12–1930)

153 CLOTHES-PRESS. Carved mahogany surmounted by a 'Chinese' fret. *About* 1760. H. 8 ft. 7 in., w. 4 ft. 6½ in. *Given by Mr E. E. Cook* (w.15–1939)

N.A.C.F. is the abbreviation for the National Art-Collections Fund

BOOKS AND DESIGNS

A large number of Contemporary Source-books, together with modern works on Georgian furniture and decoration, may be consulted in the Library of the Museum. Original designs may be seen in the Print Room of the Department of Engraving, Illustration and Design

PLATES

1 PANELLED ROOM. From No. 26 Hatton Garden, London. *About* 1730

2 PANELLED ROOM. From No. 5 Great George Street, Westminster. *About* 1750

3 THE MUSIC ROOM. From Norfolk House, St James's Square, London. *About* 1755

4 DRAWING-ROOM. From No. 5 Adelphi Terrace, London. *About* 1770

5 THE LIBRARY AT OSTERLEY PARK, MIDDLESEX. Completed in 1773

6 THE EATING ROOM AT OSTERLEY PARK. *About* 1770

7 THE TAPESTRY ROOM AT OSTERLEY PARK. Completed before 1778

8 BEDSTEAD. Carved mahogany. *About* 1740–50

BEDSTEAD. In the Chinese style. Probably made by Thomas Chippendale. *About* 1750–5

10 TABLE Carved and gilt gesso. Attributed to James Moore. Between 1714-18

11 SIDE-TABLE. Carved and gilt wood. *About* 1725

13 CHEST. Carved mahogany. *About* 1730

15 CONSOLE TABLE. Carved and gilt; marble top. *About* 1730

17 SIDE-TABLE. Carved mahogany, marble (porto-venere) top. *About* 1750

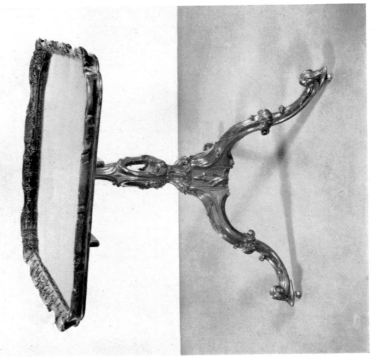

18 TABLE ON TRIPOD STAND. Carved mahogany. Mid 18th century

Right **19** TABLE ON TRIPOD STAND. ('Claw Table'). Carved mahogany. *About* 1760

21 TEA-TABLE. Carved mahogany. *About* 1760

20 READING-TABLE. Carved mahogany. Made in 1770 by William France

Above **22** CARD-TABLE. Carved mahogany. *About* 1760
Below **23** CARD-TABLE. Mahogany. *About* 1765–70

Above **24** TEA-TABLE. Mahogany. Mid 18th century
Below **25** BREAKFAST-TABLE. Mahogany (Chippendale's *Director*, 1754, Pl. xxxiii)

Above **26** TOP OF NO. 27
Below **27** SIDE-TABLE. Wood, painted and gilt. *About* 1790

Above 28 TOP OF NO. 29
Below 29 SIDE-TABLE. Painted pinewood. Irish. *About* 1790

Above **30** DRESSING-TABLE. Mahogany. *About* 1775
Below **31** WRITING-TABLE. Satinwood. *About* 1790

33 PEMBROKE TABLE. Mahogany and inlaid satinwood. *About* 1790

32 WORK-TABLE. Satinwood. *About* 1790

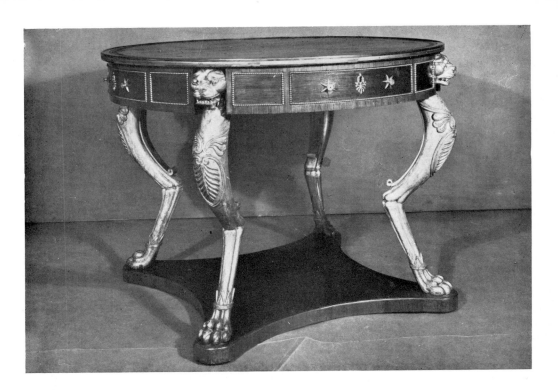

Above **34** LIBRARY TABLE. Rosewood, partly gilt. *About* 1810
Below **35** CIRCULAR TABLE (monopodium). Mahogany inlaid. Designed by Thomas Hope, 1807

36 DRESSING-TABLE. Mahogany inlaid. After a design (1805) by George Smith

37 PEDESTAL WRITING-TABLE. Carved mahogany. Made by David Wright. 1751

38 BUREAU DRESSING TABLE. Carved mahogany. Mid 18th century.

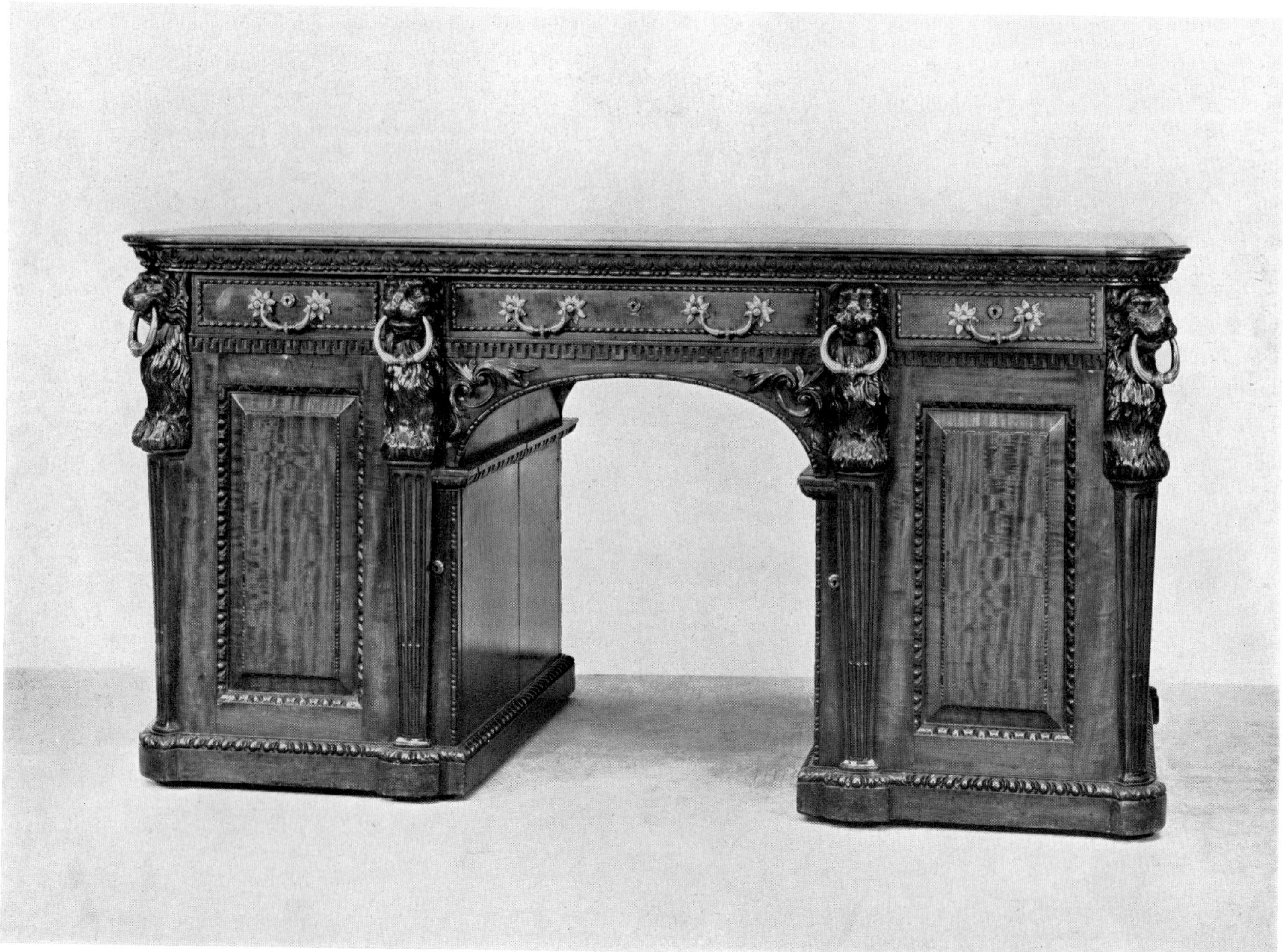

39 LIBRARY TABLE. Carved mahogany with brass mounts. 1755–60

40 LIBRARY-TABLE. Mahogany. Veneered with sabicu. *About* 1810

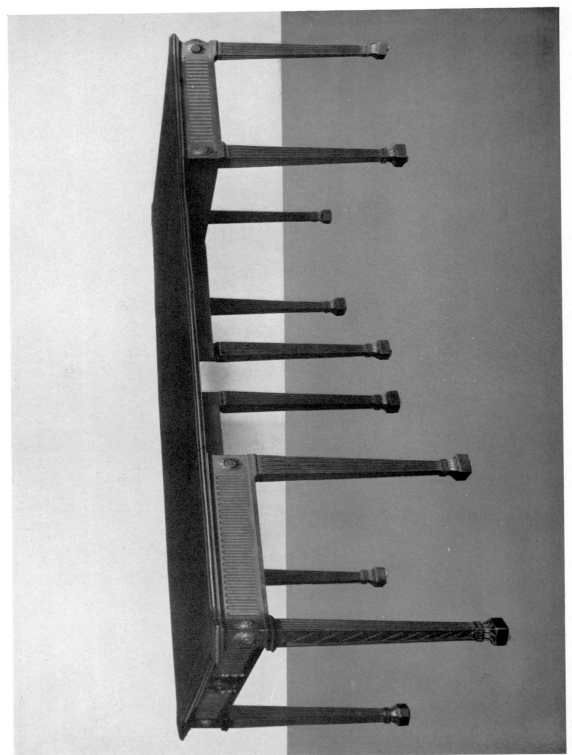

41 DINING-TABLE. Mahogany. *About* 1775

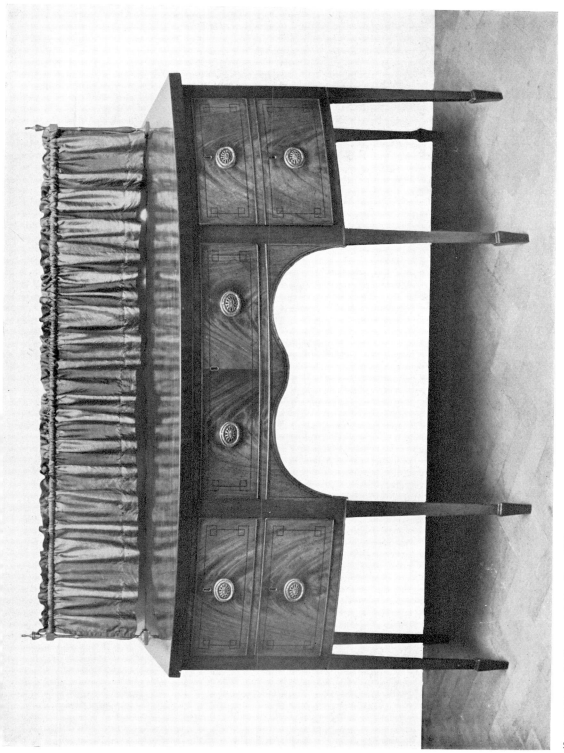

42 SIDEBOARD. Mahogany inlaid. *About* 1795

Above **43** SIDEBOARD. Mahogany. *About* 1800
Below **44** SIDEBOARD. Mahogany. *About* 1800

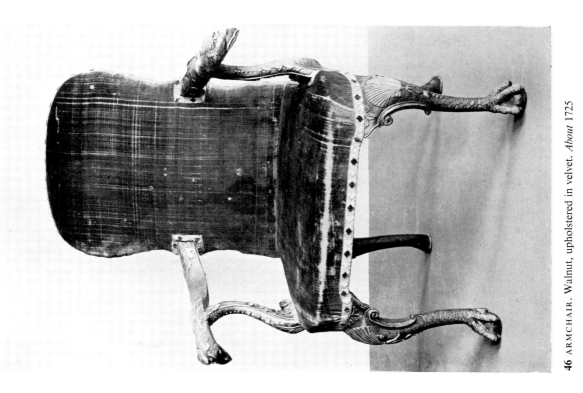

46 ARMCHAIR. Walnut, upholstered in velvet. *About* 1725

45 CHAIR. Beechwood, carved and gilt. *About* 1720

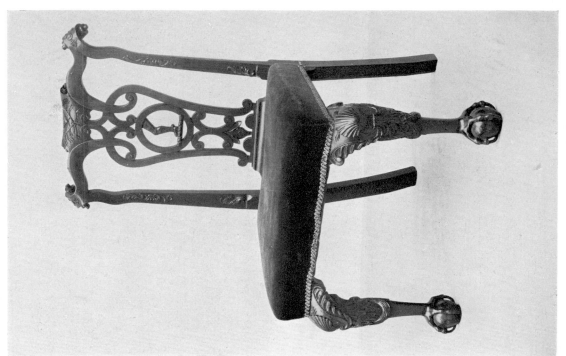

48 CHAIR. Carved mahogany. *About* 1740

47 READING CHAIR. Carved mahogany. *About* 1720

50 ARM-CHAIR. Carved mahogany. Mid 18th century.

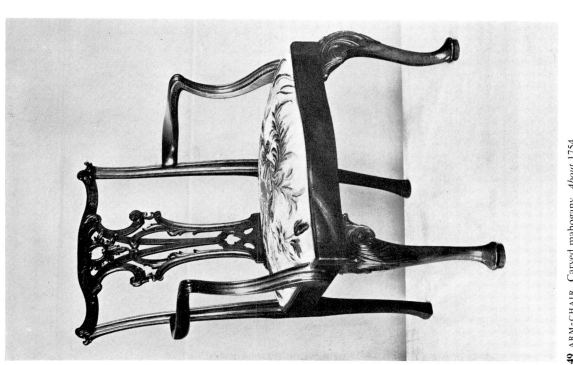

49 ARM-CHAIR. Carved mahogany. *About* 1754

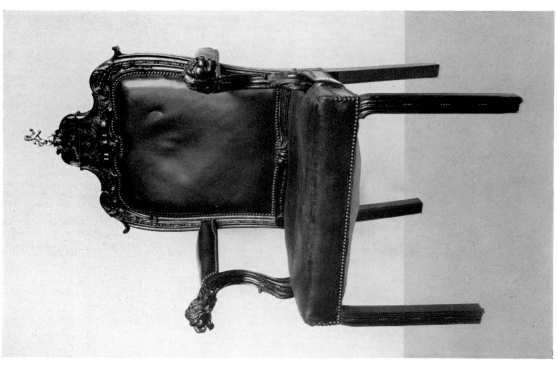

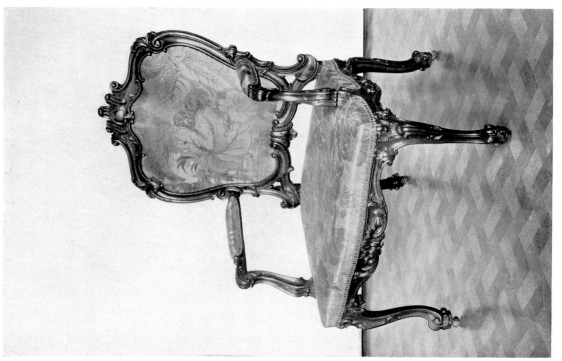

51 ARM-CHAIR. Carved mahogany. *About* 1760

52 PRESIDENTIAL ARM-CHAIR. Carved mahogany. *About* 1760

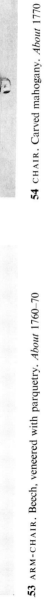

54 CHAIR. Carved mahogany. *About* 1770

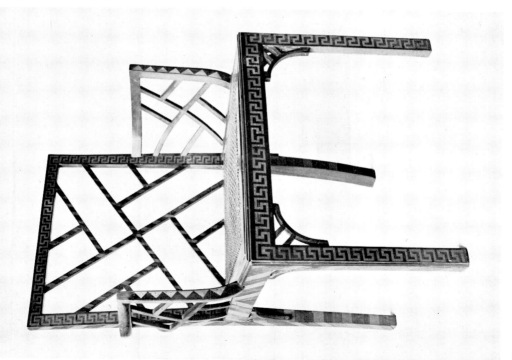

53 ARM-CHAIR. Beech, veneered with parquetry. *About* 1760–70

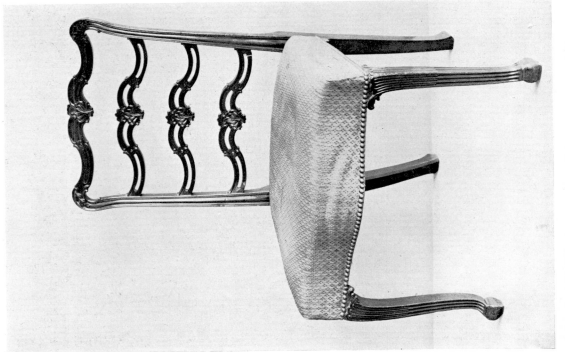

56 ARM-CHAIR. Carved mahogany. *About* 1775

55 CHAIR. Carved mahogany. *About* 1775

58 ARM-CHAIR. Carved and gilt beechwood.
Designed by Robert Adam, 1764

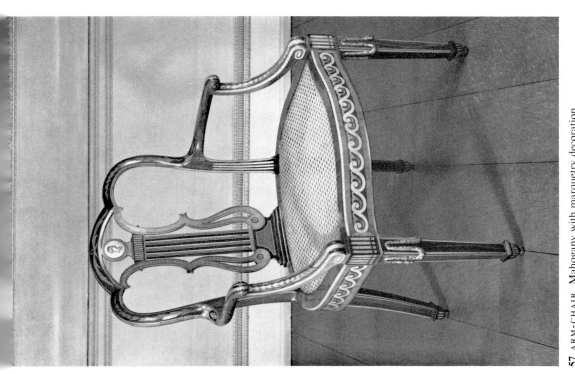

57 ARM-CHAIR. Mahogany with marquetry decoration.
Probably made by John Linnell. *About* 1770

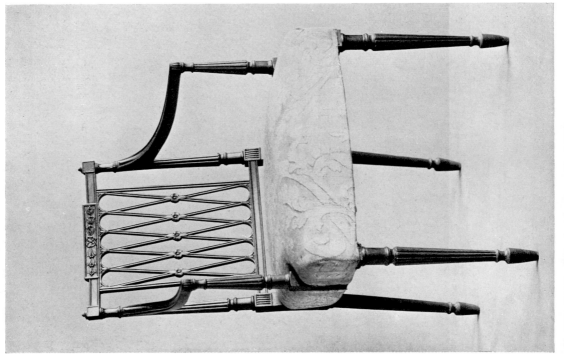

59 ARM-CHAIR. Carved mahogany. *About* 1790

60 ARM-CHAIR. Mahogany with painted decoration. *About* 1785

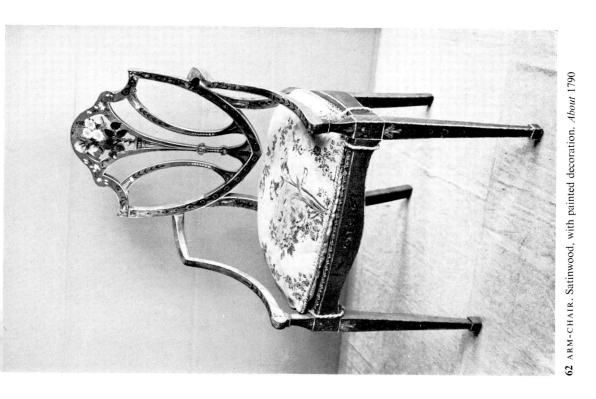

62 ARM-CHAIR. Satinwood, with painted decoration. *About 1790*

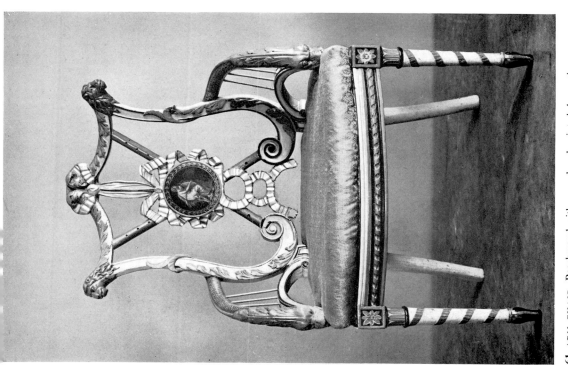

61 ARM-CHAIR. Beechwood with carved and painted decoration. *About 1778*

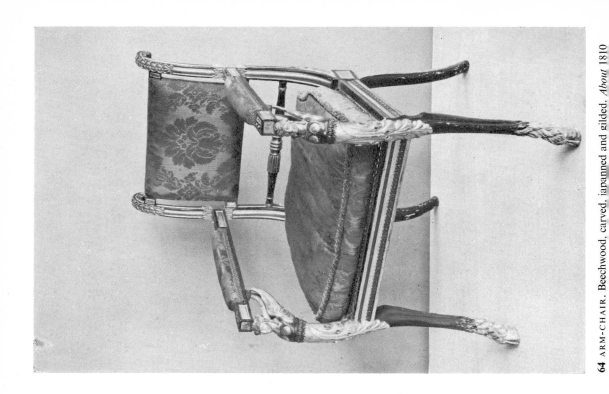

64 ARM-CHAIR. Beechwood, carved, japanned and gilded. *About* 1810

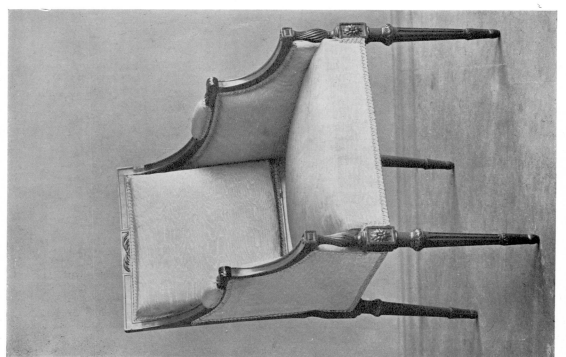

63 ARM-CHAIR. Carved mahogany. *About* 1785–90

Above **65** STOOL. Carved walnut. *About* 1720
Below **66** STOOL. Carved mahogany. Mid 18th century

67 SETTEE. Walnut with tapestry cover. Early eighteenth century

68 SETTEE. Pinewood, carved, painted and gilt. *About* 1735

69 SETTEE. Carved mahogany. *About* 1755

70 SETTEE. Carved mahogany. *About* 1755

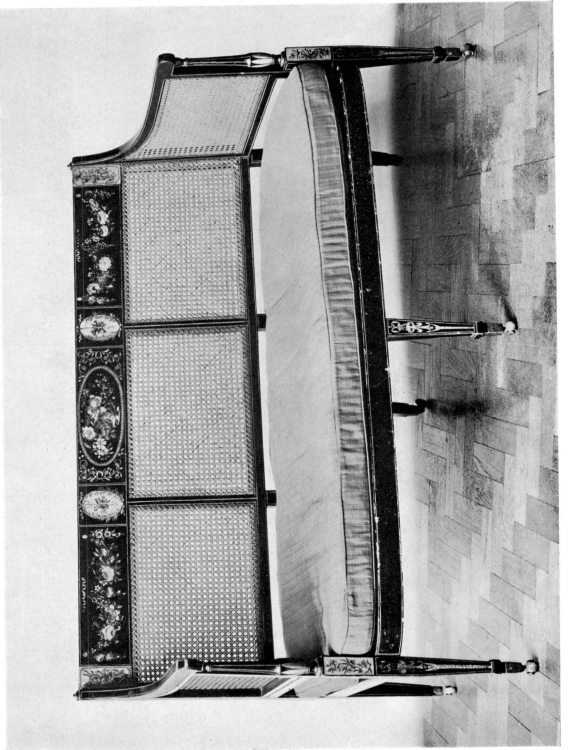

71 SETTEE. Japanned beechwood. *About* 1790

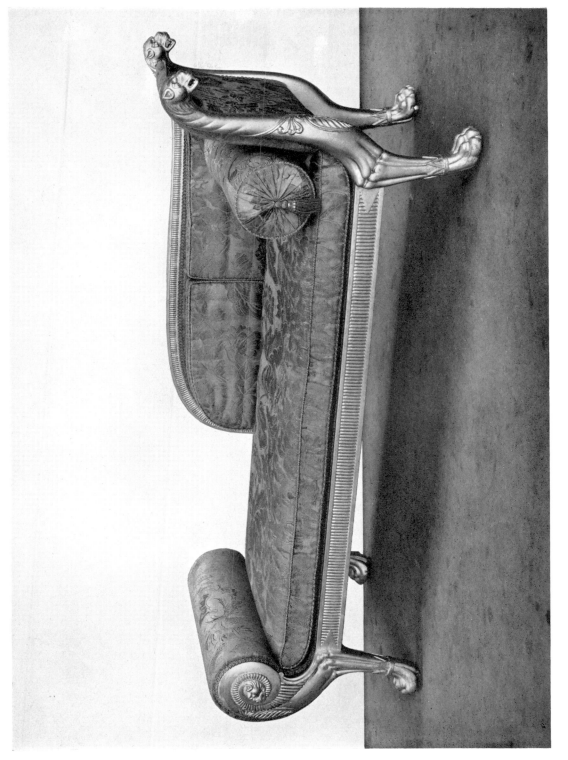

72 SETTEE. Carved and gilt beechwood. Made by Gillows, London, 1805

74 MIRROR. Carved and gilt. *About* 1730

73 MIRROR. Pinewood, carved and gilt. *About* 1740

76 MIRROR. Burr walnut, veneer and gilt gesso ornament. *About* 1730

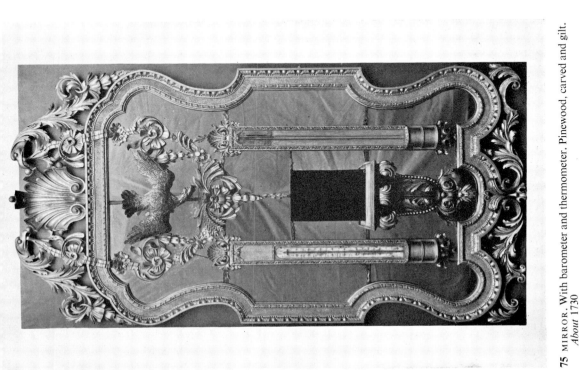

75 MIRROR. With barometer and thermometer. Pinewood, carved and gilt. *About* 1730

78 MIRROR. Mahogany veneer, partly gilt. Mid 18th century

77 MIRROR. Pinewood frame, carved and gilt. *About* 1725

79 CHIMNEY GLASS. Carved and gilt wood. Based on a design by Thomas Johnson. *About* 1760

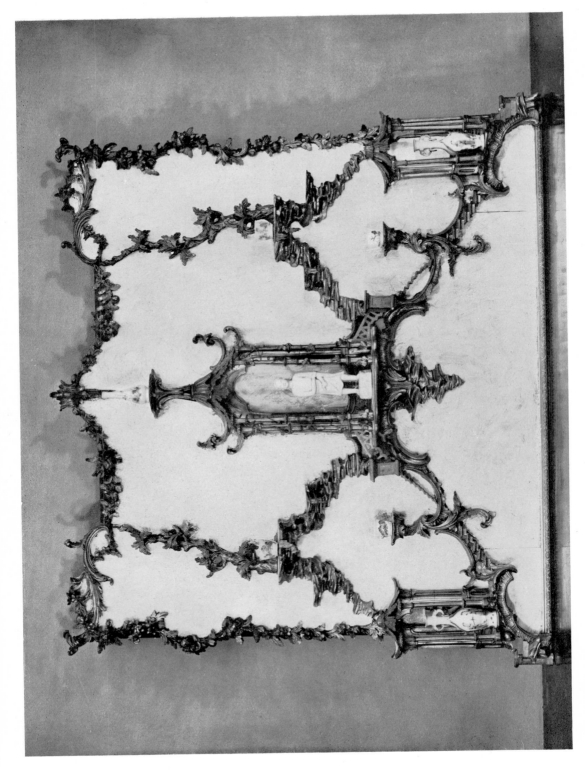

80 CHIMNEY GLASS. Carved and gilt wood. *About* 1750–60

81 MIRROR. Pinewood frame, carved and gilt. *About* 1760

82 CHIMNEY GLASS. Pinewood, carved and gilt. *About* 1774

84 MIRROR. Pinewood, carved and gilt. *About* 1810

83 MIRROR. Pinewood, carved and gilt. *About* 1800

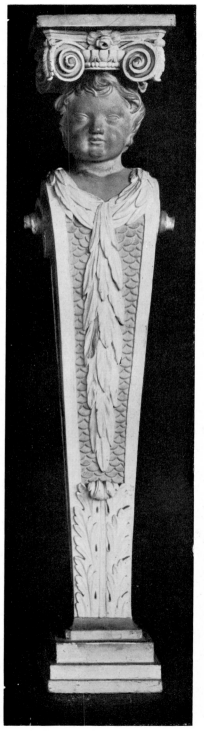

85 STAND.
  Moulded terra-cotta. *About* 1730

86 CANDLESTAND. Carved pinewood. After a design by Thomas Johnson
  About 1760–70

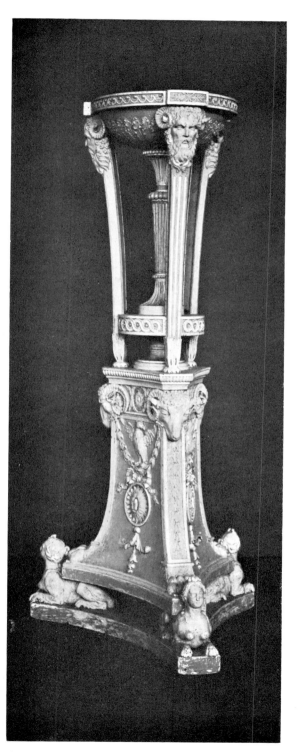

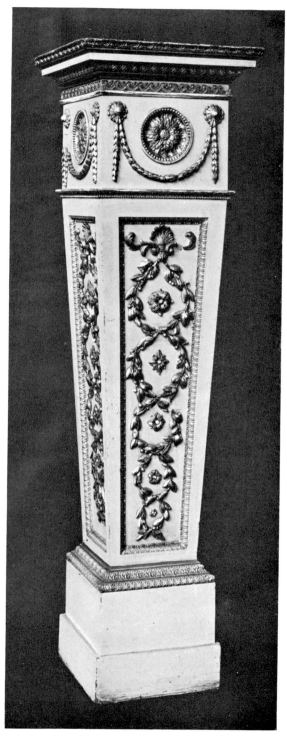

87 CANDLESTAND. Carved mahogany and pinewood, painted. *About* 1771–4

88 PEDESTAL. Wood carved, painted and gilt. Design by Robert Adam. *About* 1765

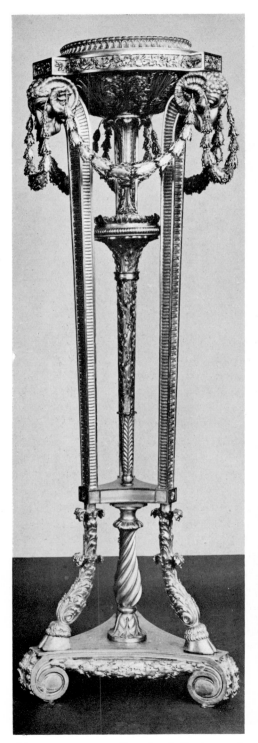

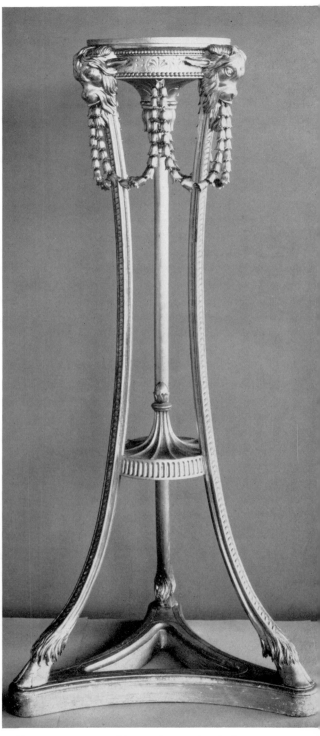

89 CANDLESTAND. Carved and gilt pinewood.
About 1770

90 CANDLESTAND. Pinewood, carved and gilt.
About 1770

91 SIDEBOARD PEDESTAL. Carved mahogany. *About* 1770

92 STAND (one of a pair). Carved mahogany. *About* 1810

93 CHANDELIER. Carved and gilt wood. *About* 1725

95 BRACKET. Carved and gilt pinewood. *About* 1760

94 BRACKET. Carved and gilt pinewood. *About* 1760

96 MIRROR WITH CANDLE BRANCHES. Carved and gilt pinewood. Designed by Robert Adam. *About* 1770

98 CANDELABRUM. Fluor-spar ('Blue John'). *About* 1765

97 WALL-LANTERN. Carved mahogany. *About* 1740

99 STAND. Carved mahogany. *About* 1760

100 ARMILLARY SPHERE. Carved mahogany; celestial sphere, brass.

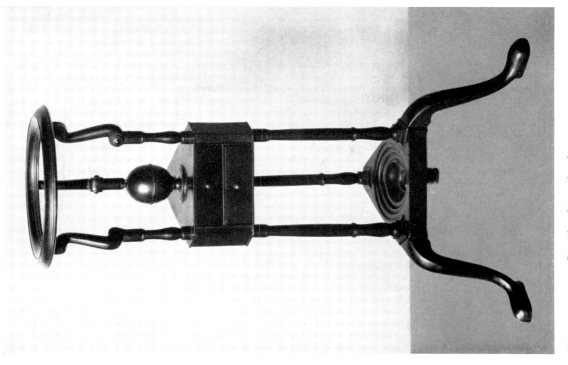

101 TERRESTRIAL GLOBE on mahogany stand. By W. and T. M. Bardin.
About 1800

102 WASHSTAND. Carved and turned mahogany.
About 1760

105 KNIFE-CASE. Satinwood, painted.
About 1790.

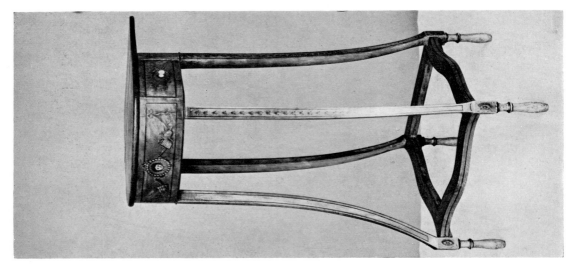

104 URN-TABLE. Satinwood with painted
decoration. About 1790.

103 TEAPOY. Rosewood with parquetry
decoration. About 1820.

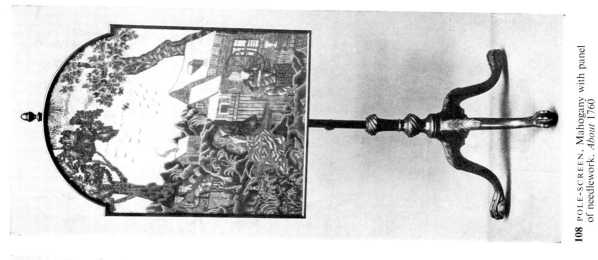

108 POLE-SCREEN. Mahogany with panel of needlework. *About* 1760

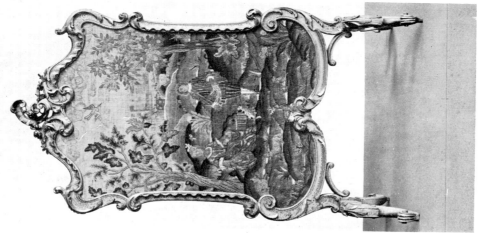

107 SCREEN. Pinewood, carved and gilt; needlework panel. *About* 1755

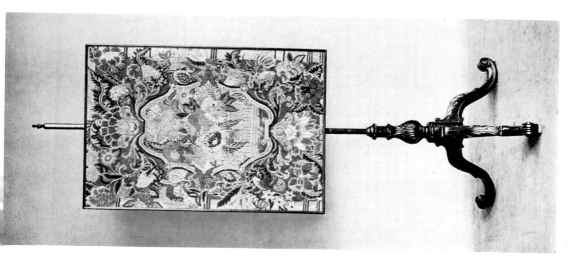

106 POLE-SCREEN. Carved mahogany with needlework panel. *About* 1760

Above **109** PAIR OF KNIFE-BOXES. Veneered with yew and inlaid. *About* 1770
Below **110** TEA-CADDIES. Inlaid (*a*) harewood; (*b*) satinwood; (*c*) walnut. *About* 1790

111 ORGAN-CASE. Carved mahogany. *About* 1760

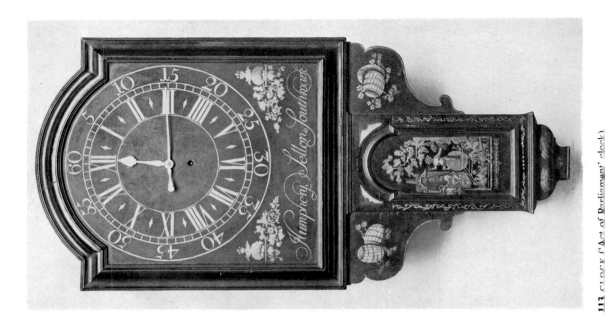

113 CLOCK ('Act of Parliament' clock)

112 HANGING CLOCK. Mahogany with applied ornaments

114 LONG-CASE CLOCK. Carved, japanned and
silvered decoration. *About* 1725

115 LONG-CASE CLOCK. Walnut veneer and
marquetry decoration. *About* 1720

116 LONG-CASE CLOCK. Carved, japanned and
silvered decoration. *About* 1725

117 LONG-CASE CLOCK. Japanned decoration.
About 1750

18 LONG-CASE CLOCK. Veneered with figured walnut. *About* 1780

119 LONG-CASE CLOCK. Mahogany with gilt-brass fittings. *About* 1775

120 LONG-CASE CLOCK. Carved mahogany. *About* 1780
121 LONG-CASE CLOCK. Mahogany inlaid with satinwood. *About* 1780

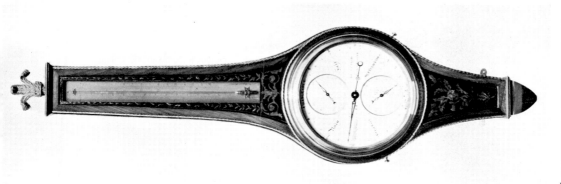

124 BAROMETER AND THERMOMETER.
Mahogany case. *About* 1800

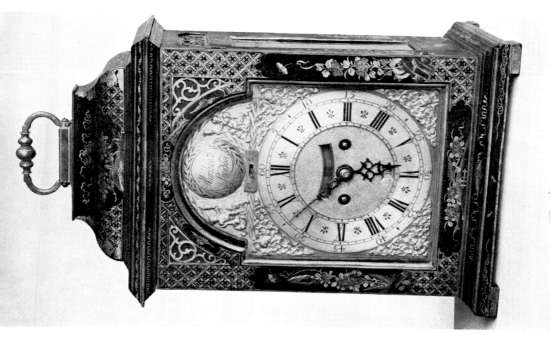

123 BRACKET CLOCK. Japanned decoration.
About 1730

122 BAROMETER AND THERMOMETER.
Carved mahogany case. *About* 1755

125 COMMODE CHEST. Carved mahogany. *About* 1760

126 DRESSING COMMODE. Mahogany inlaid. *About* 1775

127 COMMODE. Japanned decoration. *About* 1775

128 COMMODE. Veneered with Chinese lacquer. Probably designed by Robert Adam. *About* 1775

Above **129** TOP OF NO. 130
Below **130** COMMODE. Mahogany with marquetry decoration. Made by John Cobb. *About* 1775

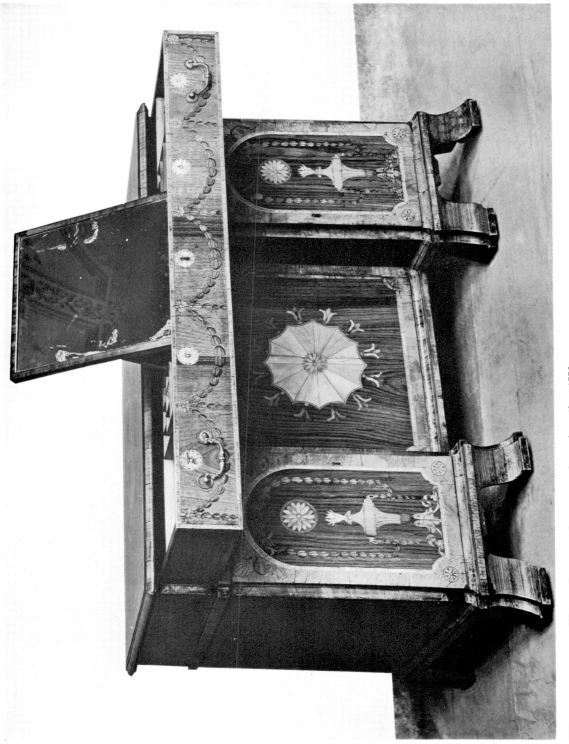

131 DRESSING-TABLE. Kingwood veneer and marquetry decoration. *About* 1775

132 COMMODE. Harewood, veneer and marquetry decoration. By William Moore of Dublin. *About 1785*

133 COMMODE. Satinwood with marquetry decoration. *About* 1775

134 COMMODE. Satinwood with painted decoration. *About* 1790

135 COMMODE. Satinwood with painted decoration. *About* 1790

136 BUREAU-CABINET. Walnut inlaid. *About* 1720

137 BUREAU-CABINET. Carved mahogany. *About* 1750

138 BUREAU-CABINET. Mahogany inlaid with brass. *About* 1730

139 CHINA CABINET. Carved mahogany. *About* 1745

140 BOOKCASE. Pinewood, carved and painted. *About* 1730

141 CABINET. Carved kingwood. 1743

142 CABINET ON STAND. Carved mahogany, enclosing a Chinese cabinet veneered with tortoiseshell. Mid 18th century.

143 CHINA CABINET ON STAND. Carved mahogany. *About* 1760

144 CABINET ON STAND. Satinwood marquetry and marble intarsia panels. Designed by Robert Adam in 1771

145 CABINET. Mahogany inlaid with satinwood. *About* 1775

146 SECRETARY-BOOKCASE. Satinwood inlaid and painted. *About* 1790

147 HANGING CABINET. Mahogany inlaid with brass. *About* 1800

148 SECRETARY. Carved satinwood. *About* 1815

149 SECRETARY. Rosewood with brass mounts. Made by John McLean and Son. *About* 1810

150 SECRETARY. Veneered with zebra-wood. *About* 1805

151 CABINET. Painted satinwood. *About* 1820

152 WARDROBE. Carved mahogany. *About* 1750

153 CLOTHES-PRESS. Carved mahogany. *About* 1760